Les McCarroll is a successful telemarketing sales manager and a co-facilitator of seminars and workshops for the rehabilitation of the unemployed and those in career transitions.

LES McCARROLL, Ed.D.

IS THERE LIFE AFTER UNEMPLOYMENT?
A Survival Guide While You Are Unemployed

A SPECTRUM BOOK

Prentice-Hall, Inc., Englewood Cliffs, New Jersey 07632

Library of Congress Cataloging in Publication Data

McCarroll, Les.
    Is there life after unemployment?

    "A Spectrum Book."
    Includes index.
  1. Job hunting. 2. Career changes. 3. Unemployed.
I. Title.
HF5382.7.437 1984   650.1'0240694   83-23096
ISBN 0-13-506015-X
ISBN 0-13-506007-9 (pbk.)

This book is available at a special discount when ordered in bulk quantities. Contact Prentice-Hall, Inc., General Publishing Division, Special Sales, Englewood Cliffs, N.J. 07632.

Editorial/production supervision: Suse L. Cioffi
Cover design © 1984 by Jeannette Jacobs
Manufacturing buyer: Edward J. Ellis

© 1984 by Prentice-Hall, Inc., Englewood Cliffs, New Jersey 07632

A SPECTRUM BOOK

ISBN 0-13-506015-X
ISBN 0-13-506007-9 {PBK.}

All rights reserved. No part of this book may be reproduced in any form or by any means without permission in writing from the publisher.

1 2 3 4 5 6 7 8 9 10

Printed in the United States of America

Prentice-Hall International, Inc., *London*
Prentice-Hall of Australia Pty. Limited, *Sydney*
Prentice-Hall of Canada Inc., *Toronto*
Prentice-Hall of India Priviate Limited, *New Delhi*
Prentice-Hall of Japan, Inc., *Tokyo*
Prentice-Hall of Southeast Asia Pte. Ltd., *Singapore*
Whitehall Books Limited, *Wellington, New Zealand*
Editora Prentice-Hall do Brasil Ltda., *Rio de Janeiro*

Contents

Acknowledgments vii

chapter one
Introduction 1

chapter two
Monday Morning Bombshell 5

chapter three
Spreading the News 13

chapter four
Encountering the Bureaucracy 25

chapter five
Surveying the Damage   49

chapter six
Starting Over   69

chapter seven
Unemployed or Unemployable?   93

chapter eight
A Look to the Future: Is There Life After Unemployment?   109

Index   120

Acknowledgments

I wish to dedicate this work to the memories of my Dad and Colby. Their help to me in spirit made so many of the feelings I describe so real. I owe a special thanks to my family, especially my wife whose support and love remained unshaking and constant. A last, heartfelt, and deeply sincere thanks go to a few very special friends who were always there to pull me when I grew weary and to push me when I got complacent. Thanks to Randy, Sue, Rick, and Jo.

chapter one

Introduction

As I recall a conversation a number of years ago, I am reminded of my enthusiasm about changing careers and having a chance to become a part-owner of a business. After seven years of working in the "helping professions," I was experiencing what is commonly referred to as "burnout." Because I had long believed that if the working climate is a healthy one, people can be happy in a host of vocations, I was not concerned about leaving a career as a counselor and psychologist to start working as a salesman. I fostered expectations of becoming financially secure and successful in a few years and my optimism only added to my success. My own training and education suggested that under normal conditions, most people probably make two or three major career transitions in a lifetime. I felt that if I were fortunate, I could get the first one out of the way at the fairly young age of twenty-nine and maybe not have to do it again.

Year after year I seemed to be performing better than adequate but no partnership emerged. It became apparent to me that this might be a pipe-dream, so I began to focus my energy on doing a better job and increasing my own earning power within the company. As it ultimately occurred, the reality of becoming so financially rewarded was probably the major factor in my now being unemployed—the company could no longer afford me. Others who had been with the company a much shorter period were retained because their salary demands were much lower.

Working in a construction-related field, a person would have to live with his or her head in the sand to not be aware of the effect of economic conditions. Ironically, as I learned that more and more of my friends and the builders I provided service for were being laid off, fired, or shut down, I marvelled at the success of our small company to stay in business. I knew our total sales were down but I also knew that our parent company could bolster our financial situation at any time and probably would to keep this young business from failing. With this knowledge, I held fast to my belief that we would come through this recession in tact and I would remain secure in my job and earnings. On a larger scale, I likened our company to a major automobile manufacturer who was rescued by the promise of government secured loans or the Wickes Corporation whose lumber yards stayed open while a Chapter 11 was being filed. If these corporations could survive, surely, I felt, so could we. So, why worry? Only "other" people were losing their jobs. Only "other" companies were going out of business. The number of unemployed included only "other" individuals, like teenagers or housewives, never the primary breadwinner such as I.

In the four to six months before losing my job, I had occasional moments of personal insecurity when I would hear a little voice inside me saying "Wake up, Les. Be prepared for the worst, because anything is possible. When push comes to shove, who do you think will be looking for a job?" Then I would reflect on the close personal relationship I had with the owner and his family and the good times we all had shared and say to myself "Forget it, everything will be alright."

Needless to say, all of my rationalizing or retreating from reality did little to retain my job. On a normal Monday morning I was informed I was being "let go." The days, weeks, and months that followed have been some of the most personally humiliating, dehumanizing, and frustrating times of my life. I found it was very paradoxical to consider myself gainfully employed when I went to sleep on a Sunday night but painfully unemployed at days end on Monday.

Obviously, mine is not a unique happening. Each day the media relates story upon story of rising unemployment, financial disasters, and increasing business failures. However, after realizing I was not dreaming and I had in fact become the "other" person, I searched for some source of support, identification, or meaning to help me through this period. Finding little, if anything, to ease my own growing fear of unemployment, financial loss, and even a ruined marriage I set about to create something of myself. This book is a result of that effort. I have intended this to be a starting point, a source of identification for others who may feel estranged or alienated from the mainstream of society because of the impact of unemployment.

From the first encounters with the unemployment office to reaffirming one's own strengths, I have tried to present this crisis in as many imaginable lights as possible. I believe the families and friends of the unemployed also suffer from this situation, and therefore included those perspectives as well. If the reality of unemployment were likened to a domino effect, I am sure we would see the fallout affecting many more than the reported numbers of unemployed. It is with this idea in mind that I have written this book for both the unemployed and those who feel they are "on the bubble" and may lose their job.

While the following account is largely a personal one, many of the examples and observations are taken from the experiences of others I encountered at the unemployment office, job service center, or welfare agency. There are a myriad of ways to lose a job as there are many ways to get another, but many of the events along the way are shared by others. This book will not tell you how to get another job but it will let you know there is a vast difference between being unemployed and being unemployable. Hopefully, after reading this book you can be a little better prepared to make the changes and pursue the avenues to become gainfully employed once again.

chapter two

Monday Morning Bombshell

How jobs are lost these days may take a variety of forms as employers attempt to be more creative in how they state the situation. Government employees may be "furloughed," teachers and educators may be part of a "reduction in force" or "RIF," automobile workers are "temporarily laid off," middle-management positions are part of a "major reorganization process," and on and on. The bottom line in all these circumstances, however, still reads the same—unemployed. Others have told me of their own insecurity in these times as they begin to realistically assess their value to a company. It seems they are painfully aware that their own job is neither as vital nor as essential to the operation of their company as it may have seemed a few short years ago. The dream of tenure has been shattered, as entire departments are abolished in reorganization plans at colleges and universities. Years ago, mechanization and computer technology were seen as major threats to many long-standing jobs in the marketplace. That threat never materialized to the degree anticipated, but today's unemployment is a reality occurring in numbers never before seen in this country.

Working for a relatively small business, I was oblivious to how people were having their employment terminated or how they were being informed of it. The Friday before losing my own job, it was business as usual. After reaching the point of being able to effectively manage the business alone for short periods, I felt this offered the owner a great deal of freedom to spend time away from the business with his family. So, this was just another three or four-day vacation for him while I took care of the office. Years ago, he would always "check in" to see how things were going but that was no longer necessary. We would, however, try to touch base on the night before he would return to work for any messages, appointments, or similar notes. Sunday was no exception as I visited him and his family after their camping trip. We talked for quite a while about business and personal concerns and I left with the feeling that nothing was awry. Payroll, scheduling, and warehouse activities were all in order and on time. The only thing he had to take care of was disciplining a new employee who was becoming a problem for him.

Monday morning started off as normally as any other. It had long been a procedure for one of us to come in fifteen or twenty minutes after the other. This was because the other employees would often try to get different stories from us on the same problem and use that as a reason to not do the assigned work. If only one of us was there when they got their work orders, there was much less confusion and procrastination. So, I followed the owner in by twenty minutes and the other office staff came later.

It occurred to me since then how naive I must have been not to know what was coming, but I have discovered that many others have experienced the same feeling of being the last one to know what was about to happen. I can recall humorous conversations with the owner about other employees who were fired. I remember that it was important to find a creative way to have an employee quit instead of firing him or her so unemployment benefits could not be collected. Having never been in a position to fire anyone, these stories were always a bit alien to me but the disdain with which a fired employee was regarded never set very well with me. I see little humor in trying to devise ways to have someone quit a job or in the fact that everyone else in the company may know who is being fired before that person actually knows. After a firing, it seemed there was always an outpouring of how that employee had messed up so many details and was solely responsible for the loss of large sums of money. I suppose these conversations occur at many levels and at a number of other companies but it seems to me to be a very unhealthy view of employees and the working relationship with them.

There are many ways for a person to discover they no longer have a job. Some get the infamous "pink slip" in their pay envelope, others may receive a computerized form letter telling them of the economic hard times and the resulting necessary layoffs, and still others may learn through media releases of a mine or plant closing. Small business owners sometimes choose to inform the employee through the secretary or other third party or perhaps by withholding job assignments. Occasionally, the boss will do the firing, as was my experience.

I began to leave the office for an appointment and was asked to wait a moment to talk briefly with the owner. Because this was a very common request over the years, I felt certain he wished to ask my opinion on some sales or personnel issue. I was correct about the personnel issue, but was ill-prepared for the nature of the conversation. After a futile attempt to ease into the heart of the problem the owner finally blurted out "I'm letting you go." At that point, I recall a very deliberate and rehearsed speech that included many platitudes of praise and regret. At issue for him was not the friendship and closeness developed over the years, but making this difficult decision in light of impending financial pressures placed on him by two major factors. The first, and most obvious, was the decreasing level of sales as a result of a dramatic drop in homebuilding. The second, unspoken and subtle source of pressure, was maintaining a highly inflated salary schedule for himself and another family member in the company. After discussing the financial woes of his small business and assuring me that the firing was not a result of any personal or professional shortcomings, the conversation became even more mechanical. He quickly outlined the financial considerations of severance pay and any unused vacation, then moved to returning sales journals and materials. He finally apologized once again. End of saga!? Not quite.

My initial reaction was disbelief followed closely by a sense of relief, which was followed more closely by a feeling of hopelessness. Many viable alternatives crystallized in my mind to alleviate the pressures he felt and thus prevent my firing. But before I could voice any of them I stopped myself and decided that if I was being fired, I would be damned if I would provide any insights for changing the economic complexion of that business! All for one, and one for all! My sense of disbelief centered on some irrational notion that because we had been so close for so long, he would at least let me fail with the company if it was, in fact, going to fail. My senses were wrong because as he stated, "This is nothing personal, it's being done in hope of saving the company." His approach was economic, mine was human. I'm sure not one person in a hundred would consider my view a very prudent business position, but it was, nonetheless, my position at the time of firing. Needless to say, my ideas have changed since then.

The sense of relief I experienced was that the anticipation was finally over for me. The constant focus on the national recession, business failures, the downturn of homebuilding and our accompanying drop in sales, had created an overly pessimistic view of the future for me. Each time my company was not selected to do some work, I felt personally responsible. As stated earlier this relief was short-lived. Within one hour, an overwhelming feeling of hopelessness or despair began to swell within me as the reality of the situation sank in.

In reflecting back on what happened and the hours that followed, I have been able to distinguish my more general feelings and reactions about being fired. First, and foremost, while letting me go may have been difficult for the owner, the inescapable truth was that it was he who would still have a job, a paycheck, a place to go each day and, more importantly, a feeling of job security. On the other hand, I lost all of those things in an instant. I was the one left floundering and in a state of shock. My defensive instincts made me question the worthiness of other workers who were not being released. I also wanted to explore alternatives. But my questioning only led to the realization that the decision had been made and it was final. Indeed, there was no "court of appeals" to hear well-developed arguments for retaining my services. I remain awed at the ease of letting someone go when placed in a purely economic frame. The only governing factor in the entire process is the necessity of the business to survive. Alternatives are rarely explored when expedience is the goal. Undoubtedly, a loyal and effective employee represents an uncomfortable dilemma when sales are down and salaries are up. Others have indicated to me their own feelings of insecurity with large corporations because of their own rising salaries. Merit raises and cost-of-living increases are nice, but they may be part of a double-edged sword. The facts seem to indicate that the fastest way to cut overhead is to reduce or eliminate high salaries. Given the tenor of the times, this fact can be very disquieting even for those individuals with many years of service to a company. I sometimes wonder if I might still be employed if I would have turned down the annual cost-of-living pay increases and thus been more "affordable." I believe economic justifications are usually cop-outs and given because of their ease of rationalizing. A more difficult and challenging course would certainly be to devise ways to retain valuable employees. Although these alternatives would appear to be nonexistent in the instances of perhaps a Chrysler Corporation or a Braniff Airlines, I am certain numerous smaller businesses have choices open that are never explored or even considered.

It seems ironic that if the current situation is viewed purely from the corporate position, employees may actually be responsible for their own unemployment because they have accepted pay increases and benefits over the years. It would seem that large unions must also bear some of the blame for the situation. With all of this rationalizing, I still find one, very consistent reality. I am the one unemployed—not the union negotiators or the higher salaried executives. I am the one with no paycheck going to the unemployment office, not the corporate comptroller who evaluated profits and losses or the owners' son who can never seem to complete one simple task before launching into five others.

Drawing both from my own experience and the descriptions of others, I have noticed a recurring phenomenon which is quite interesting. Because the justification for the firing is purely a business consideration and not at all personal, there is a tendency to view the exemployee-boss relationship as unchanged or certainly still amiable. Some people continue to visit their old bosses and coworkers—even on days when they are out looking for a new job! While I have had little, if any, interaction with my past employer, I am very aware of my own curiosity, perhaps morbid, about the business and the other employees who remained. I suppose a long and involved psychological explanation could be offered for these feelings, but this is neither the time nor place for such a discussion. It remains that there is a large void created when a person loses his or her job and filling it can be an emotionally arduous task.

When viewing employment exclusively in terms of black or red ledger entries, it seems very logical that there should be financial considerations given to "reduction in force" employees, particularly because there are no other considerations to be given. These may range from reimbursement for unused vacation or sick pay to extended severance pay. Here again, however, the bottom line reads the same—unemployed. Severance pay, vacation pay, or even undeclared gifts of cash serve only the guilt-ridden ends of the employer and are, at best, a temporary bandage for a severe wound. On examination it appears even the insurance companies are trying to capitalize on the plight of the unemployed by offering continued benefits to a fired employee privately but at much higher premiums. Some insurance companies even offer short-term coverage labeled specifically for the unemployed. As I recalled past conversations with my boss describing the tactics used for withholding profit-sharing checks much longer than necessary or trying to delay unemployment benefits, I suddenly realized I was lucky to be getting any financial considerations at all! After all, on a large scale, a corporation paying high interest rates on borrowed funds may save enormous sums of money by earning another 30 or 60 days of interest payments on substantial amounts. How can the unemployed do anything more than wait?

My final considerations about being fired center around the process of severing all ties with the company. Using the leverage of withholding my final paycheck, I was asked to turn in any keys, files, records, or materials I had that the company owned. Having seen the door locks changed every time a person quit or was fired over a five-year period, I knew that even giving a key back would not ease the fears of my old boss that I might retaliate in some way. In the past, lawsuits had been threatened to have meaningless invoices returned so I was sure I would not be allowed any slight indiscretion in this area. By the time a person is being fired, qualities of loyalty and honesty are quickly forgotten and a posture of self-defense is immediately assumed by the employer and maintained through the entire episode. This begins with the final notice of employment and lasts until the "door hits you on the way out." Fortunately, because a company wishes to return to normalcy and a fired employee is considered a leper away from the colony, this entire process goes very quickly. For me, from the words "I'm letting you go" to the bartering of my final check for a key, only a couple of hours were involved. For others I've spoken with, the process has been much quicker, but a few others had to endure protracted conflict to gain either a final check or unemployment benefits. The most dehumanizing statement made by my employer during the conversation of being fired, however, was an intimation for future consideration "if the economy picks up."

chapter three

Spreading the News

Dealing with the immediate feelings of losing a job is a very difficult necessity. This difficulty increases greatly because of the lack of any real "mourning" period. There is an immense difference between fearing or fantasizing the loss of a job and finding yourself unemployed. A swelling of anger and hostility aided by a strong sense of powerlessness must be brought under control in order to let life go on. The initial impact of being fired is usually absorbed directly by the employee while the residual affects permeate family and friends who surround him or her.

The two biggest decisions I had to make in the hours following my firing, were when and how to inform my family and friends. Because I felt as though I had failed as a provider of financial and emotional security, I had serious misgivings about how I would be perceived by my family. My fear was that they would begin to view me as I now viewed myself. Would my family still consider me worthy of love? Was I, indeed, a failure and inadequate as a provider? As these questions arose, I also wondered how I would feel if my wife lost her job. Being a "second" income my tendency had been to discount its importance. But after losing my employment, I recognized the obvious financial advantages of her working and also realized that I had not been very appreciative of second income jobs—until now. This, however, only served to increase my own anxiety as I now questioned my value to my wife. After all, without a job, I felt I would no longer have a right to determine how money should be spent or what activities should be engaged in. I lost my credibility and power in the relationship. Fortunately, there is little time to do very much of this thinking before the reality of the situation again emerges and family and friends must be told what has happened. The fears and anxiety do not disappear, however, but merely recede as more immediate concerns demand to be dealt with.

Effect of Unemployment on Marriage

Having seen the destructive impact of unemployment on families and friendships in the past, I was hopeful in trying to move through this period with as little emotional damage as possible. The financial fallout seemed so wide range, I felt unable to anticipate all the affects. While just weeks before, having children was an immediate goal and wish, pregnancy now became a feared event and a threat to economic stability or what remained of it. The fear of a difficult pregnancy and a potential loss of needed income, was so great that even sexual behavior changed. Coupled with an increasing need for a spouse to keep working, it is clear that a marriage must withstand a great deal during these times. Some people may say that these are the times which strengthen bonds of marriage and increase the appreciation of husbands and wives for each other, but personally I can imagine many other ways to enhance my marriage relationship without needing the insecurity produced by unemployment.

Everything from work pressures to sexual needs may be affected, but when considering the complexities of life there must also be other changes. From a financial perspective, a long-awaited and well-planned family vacation will probably have to be placed on the back burner. If reservations and timed vacations were involved, the trip may have to be cancelled altogether. Major or needed remodeling is out of the question and continuing to use those nearly worn out appliances or automobiles is a must. Large purchases are suicidal, but small spending suffers also. Normal social or recreational activities are scrutinized carefully and activities at home are given priority. God-forbid that a television would ever fail during this time! All of these things add tremendous pressures to a marriage relationship. Even the most stable relationships may bend severely under such forced changes and less secure ones probably break.

Given these circumstances it is not unusual to see changes in a husband or wife. With a husband losing a job, the wife is placed in a position of having to provide the income for necessities. If she happens to be a career-oriented professional this is probably not difficult. However, if she has typically been the source of revenue for "extras," this new role of primary or sole supporter can be most uncomfortable. I gather from my own experience and the observation of others, when a wife loses her job the husband sees only the financial implications and typically remains unaware of deeper emotional damage that may be occurring. From this standpoint, again, a wife generally must experience a greater sense of loss when her husband is released than he does if she loses her job. Perhaps this is another example of the pervasive chauvinism in the male population today.

The frustration of being helpless to change either the employer or the economy may lead to a deep sense of anger and hostility toward the immediate cause of such frustration

—namely the owner and the company. As an analogy, it seems only natural that if there were a large thorn in a person's side causing great pain and discomfort he or she would certainly remove it and probably curse the reason for it being there. Such may be the reaction of a spouse who is forced to be a sole provider where she previously had been either unemployed or only a secondary provider. Quite naturally, if a long-awaited vacation or major remodeling project must be abandoned, resentment is likely to exist. Couple these circumstances with a deep loss of personal security, and it is clear to see that changes do occur that must be contended with if the marriage itself is to survive.

When the initial shock and negative feelings are resolved, the marriage partner, either husband or wife, may become a tremendous emotional asset in reorganizing and restructuring the other's life. A spouse can give understanding, compassion, and encouragement when no one else can. Even interim financial stability is a vitally important issue when a person is starting over and may be able to provide only a small share of the money needed to meet a family's obligations.

When informing my wife, who works full-time as a teacher, of losing my job, I was met with two reactions almost immediately. The first was total disbelief and a need for more details or explanation. The second, which recurs periodically, was anger and hostility. It was remarkable to me that only hours before, she had a secure feeling about our future, children, a vacation, and her own retirement, but in one sentence, all of those thoughts were erased and substituted with so much resentment. As expressed earlier, the negative feelings for me are not necessarily gone, but more under control while I continue to piece together a new sense of direction and purpose. In the meantime, I contend with the anger of my wife and try to accept its nature.

Effect of Unemployment on Children

For the children of unemployed parents, a great deal of anxiety exists. The very young probably experience no difficulty if their basic needs are still being met and as long as their world is comprised primarily of brothers or sisters. There is, however, a strong likelihood that parents who are too preoccupied with finding a new job or making ends meet, will not have either the time or inclination to respond to a wide range of children's needs. In this respect, even very young children will experience a change in the nature of the relationship with one or both parents. In addition, older children who must encounter peers each day are under a very different set of pressures. Adolescents may experience embarrassment when forced to answer a prospective boy- or girlfriend's question of "What does your father do?," or "Where do your folks work?" They also feel a loss of security and stability in their own lives as they seek to discover how their needs are going to be met. While skipping a prom or homecoming may seem like an insignificant event to an adult, most assuredly it can be devastating to a youngster, particularly if the only reason for missing it is because a parent lost his or her job. This disappointment is in turn felt by a parent and only adds to his or her own sense of failure. Once again, the lives of so many seem to be disrupted by the inability of one person to keep a job.

After the initial shock is alleviated by some discussion of how things must change for at least the time being, older children are likely to either ask how they can or tell how they will help out. Many will try to get part-time work and give the money to the family or provide for their own personal needs. Still others may take the lead and examine ways to cut out spending an allowance, or wasting food, energy, or clothing. Children can be as rich a source of support during this period as a good spouse. Empathetic toward parents by nature, children are able to give their acceptance and trust unconditionally, thus showing their love for a parent during this ordeal.

Effects of Unemployment on the Parents of the Unemployed

Parents of unemployed persons are another component of the family group to be considered. Their situation is similar to that of their grandchildren in that they too may feel embarrassed when asked by their friends what a son or daughter does for a living. Just a few days earlier the response was probably given quickly and with a certain sense of pride. Now the answer is given with three or four justifying or explanatory statements. A thriving source of self-satisfaction has been dashed by the reality of unemployment. Similarly, as children experience a loss of stability, so too may parents who have viewed their son or daughter as successful, financially secure and potentially able to help them as they grow older and require various forms of nursing care. How can someone help who has no financial resources to work with? This loss of security is not only in a financial sense. Older parents who have grown accustomed to regular visits or extended time with grandchildren and perhaps even a regular allowance from their children, can become very uneasy about the prospect of their child having to move in order to locate new work or having to sell a home because payments can no longer be made. For parents who themselves have experienced the Great Depression, these fears will not easily subside.

Under certain conditions where a child may have had to move back in with his or her parents and perhaps bring a young family along, a parent might have to legally sever ties in order for the child to qualify for government benefits. This severing may mean the loss of free room and board or, in fact, having them move out. Surely, this is an exception but it is another example of the effects of unemployment in today's world. From a purely pragmatic point of view, parents can represent a last bastion of hope for the unemployed. Though they may not be able to provide a job, they may certainly be in a position to offer financial help and, just as important, emotional strength through acceptance and encouragement.

The family can have a dramatic and powerful effect on how a person deals with his or her own crisis of unemployment. Even though all of the family members experience the negative affects of this crisis, the ultimate responsibility for changing it lies with the unemployed individual. I am certain not all of us who are without a job right now are surrounded by beautifully compassionate and understanding families willing to do anything to help ease our pressure. On the other hand, by understanding the feelings of all concerned, family members can learn to pull together in order to survive the times intact. Not every wife will want to stay with a man she considers a failure. Not all children will understand why there is no money for a homecoming suit or gasoline for the car. Not all parents will have either the resources or inclination to help their child. With or without this support, however, the situation remains the same—unemployed.

Telling Your Friends

Before actually telling any of my personal friends about losing my job, I recalled how "bad news has a way of traveling fast." I had a fairly good idea that if I informed a couple of key people, they would certainly see that others were made aware of my "situation." I was certain that many people would call for me at work and find out from someone there that I had been fired. I had a sense of what to expect when my friends found out because I had encountered this a number of times before when mutual friends had lost their jobs.

Within the first week, there was an outpouring of regrets and sympathy about my loss. I heard stories of how poorly one friend's job was going and he wanted to quit. Another friend just got a new boss who was changing a lot of things and reorganizing the personnel so he was feeling insecure about his job too. A third friend feared being reclassified and demoted only a few years before retirement. I could appreciate all of this input and support but I somehow felt as though this was not happening for my benefit alone. I sensed a need on the part of friends to reaffirm the nature of our relationship now that I was unemployed. Some were curious about how I would react socially. Would I be cynical, depressed, hostile? Or, would I become a recluse and reject their offers of help? For some, I became an instant failure or, at best, a very large source of anxiety. The crisis of being unemployed was made too real for some as they reviewed their own sense of job security.

Aside from instances of overt patronizing, friends can be very helpful during times like these. I found I didn't need to have an axe to grind for my old employer, some of my friends did it for me. They were incredulous that I would be released after all I did for that company! Friends also can demean the entire social and economic spectra that have caused such a thing. Though these reactions may help bolster a deflated ego for a brief period, they never quite erase that sense of loss experienced in being let go. It must be difficult to imagine that when a person loses a job, not every waking moment is spent either condemning the culprit or contemplating the outcome. It seems to be that friends sometimes forget that before unemployment there might have been a myriad of things to discuss without one of them being about how to find a new job.

I seem to notice that some people need to be able to categorize others so they can better understand them. However, when no job or occupation exists as a label, a great deal of anxiety is created. After all, if you ask what I do for a living and I reply "nothing," how do you interpret that? How can you categorize me? If I answer "butcher," you plug it right in and we talk about knives or beef or groceries. Have you ever tried to plug in "nothing?" What do we talk about then? Some people need to label us; it provides security for them.

Friends may provide a rich source of job referrals. Everyone has an idea or solution for the problem. "Have you been here?" or "Have you talked to so-and-so?", "I hear they are hiring out there" or, finally, "I cut this out of the want ads for you, have you seen it?" Under these circumstances patience is indeed a virtue. Friends want nothing more than for you to return to the way you were—working at something, at anything! Things can never be as they were, however. They may improve, they may get worse. But they will never be the same!

Last, it must be kept in mind that friends offer an opportunity for the unemployed to view life as it should be—as functioning, involved people. If a circle of friends includes only others who are unemployed, there can be a real danger of getting into patterns of feeling sorry for oneself or complaining about one's life situation without trying to change it. Support groups can be very good if they foster positive and functional growth. If they do not, they should be avoided. Be aware of personal friends who may bring out only the negative feelings in you and also those who may offer support and genuine encouragement. With this awareness, choose how and with whom you will spend time.

From time to time over the past few years, I have had conversations with friends about other people who got laid off or fired from their jobs. Usually, one person would say that it was too bad, someone else would add a searching question about what they would do for a job or money, and finally someone would conclude that everything would work out. The unspoken truth by us all was that we were glad it didn't happen to us. Such, I believe, was the case when I lost my job. My colleagues and coworkers were very shocked at my release because they knew of the long-standing personal relationship with the owner and his family. They also knew of the high quality of my own work over the period of my employment. Their disbelief, however, quickly changed to apprehension about their own future with the company. Their concern shifted from wondering "if" they would lose their job, to "when" would they lose it. The firing of a long-standing and loyal employee has a very disquieting affect on the remaining workers. After seeing others lose their jobs, I would wonder if I was doing the right things in terms of work-quality and attitude to ensure my own continued employment. This self-questioning invariably led to a personal reassessment and sometimes reaffirmation of goals, values, and attitudes.

The relieved feeling that someone else lost their job instead of you is only temporary as the reality of the situation emerges. The fact is that the same thing might happen to you. My friends and I would, from time to time, evaluate our jobs in relation to an "economic war zone." Construction-related occupations were the advance troops with no back-up support; middle-management personnel with high salaries were on the front lines; personnel officers were the support troops always under fire; tenured professors were the main line of defense; and owners and their relatives were at command headquarters removed from the danger. It isn't difficult to see where all of the casualties take place in this kind of war!

In order to ease the sense of insecurity under the conditions described, colleagues would often go through a process of denial–entrenchment–disassociation. They would deny the actual weakness of their company and the economy in order to show how well the business was faring. They would entrench themselves more deeply into the company by overstating their own vital role in the continued success of the business. Finally, they would disassociate their vulnerability by choosing to believe a coworker was let go for reasons such as poor work quality, bad attitude or inability to perform under pressure. I can recall vividly a caricature picture on a wall at my last job that stated if anything was wrong or missing, it was the fault of the person last fired. I wonder how much humor that picture holds for people who are unemployed like myself.

Some interesting points to consider occurred to me a short time after being let go. For instance, if a person wants to continue in the same or a closely related field of work, wouldn't maintaining membership in affiliated professional groups and organizations be a good idea? Apart from the cost of memberships and dues, these could be good resources for jobs and information. But I believe it might seem odd to be at a plumber's convention if I were no longer employed as a plumber, or at a teacher's gathering if I were not teaching. Again, while I might be just a casual friend to many of the people or members of these organizations, I am also a walking, talking, and breathing reminder that it could happen to them. In that sense I'm sure I create a certain amount of discomfort and anxiety within them. From my viewpoint, if "nothing breeds success like success" then I certainly want to stay involved with these groups. On the other hand, from the standpoint of those still successfully employed, I might be the catalyst that changes the motto to read "nothing breeds failure like failure."

chapter four

Encountering the Bureaucracy

As the dust begins to settle on the initial traumas of becoming unemployed and letting others know of the situation, the next major hurdle of life usually involves some component of the government bureaucracy. Just as a newborn baby may nurse at its mother's breast for life sustenance, the recently unemployed individual often embarks on a relationship with a series of departments, agencies, offices, and institutions that will become the sole providers of financial or vocational support. Such a dependent existence may continue for an extensive period of time. To a person who has had some experience dealing with a bureaucracy, this may not be too uncomfortable emotionally or psychologically. However, for the naive or inexperienced this can be a brutal and dehumanizing occurrence.

THE SYSTEM

In order to gain some insight into the "system," a few brief observations are in order that may explain the functioning characteristics of various government offices or agencies. First, and foremost, it must be understood that the bureaucracy is like a living, breathing, fully functioning organism. Its ultimate aim is in self-perpetuation. In this sense, its own needs must first be provided for in order to initiate services for any clients. While it is true that many agencies serve the sick, needy, destitute, handicapped, or unemployed very nobly, there should be no mistaking that these concerns are secondary. The lifeblood of any bureaucracy is money, or an operating budget, generally provided through government funding. Normally, the level of funding is determined through a combined analysis of documented needs based on past performance, anticipated client levels, and the demonstrated successful delivery of services. Of these three, success is the most critical. Because of the close relationship of success ratio to ultimate financial support, agencies are forced to be somewhat creative in either their reporting of or their criteria for success. Through careful and calculated reporting, each department or office can be assured of obtaining at least as much funding as the previous year if the comparisons are the same and potentially more if the numbers suggest a dramatic increase in need. The important thing to remember, however, is that reduced funding generally means reduced services but increased funding only means that the staff is increased. In either instance, the needs of the clients are relegated to second, and sometimes third or fourth, best.

Rate of Success

Having worked within the government bureaucracy for many years, I was able to observe some of the strange methods used for determining success and the equally odd techniques for reporting it. It was not uncommon for as many as three agencies to claim a "success" for the same client as each might have provided some service to that person. Likewise, it was not uncommon for an agency to try to "unload" a client with a poor prognosis of success on another agency. The end result is understandable if it is kept in mind that each office needed to maintain, at minimum, its status quo and this was done primarily through the documentation of successful implementation of programs or services. For example, an unemployed, handicapped, social security recipient may represent high probability of success if the primary services needed are a training program and some tools and then placement. In this case, a welfare agency, vocational rehabilitation, and a social security office might all claim a success. On the other hand, if the probability of success appears very low, each office will likely try to refuse their services or limit them because of a poor prognosis. It should be noted that often this potential for success is very subjective and there may be no written documents to substantiate such a position. This protects each agency from a potential discrimination lawsuit and, once again, tends to diminish the probability of showing a lower ratio of success.

I note this example to demonstrate that there would appear, at times, to be no logical way of understanding the bureaucracy short of becoming as fragmented and illogical as it is. Keeping in mind that each agency tends to want to work independently, there may even be some potential short-term benefits for the clients. Because there are so many civil servants in these bureaucracies, the odds of something positive happening are probably increased due to the fact that there must be a number of genuinely conscientious, caring people working within the system. It might also occur that services are duplicated from time to time. Though this is ultimately discovered and corrected, the immediate effect may be very good for the recipient.

Agencies—Then and Now

In comparing the way agencies functioned in the late sixties and early seventies to what may now be found some major distinctions in both the attitudes and the abilities of the civil servants can be observed. There are certainly a number of valid causes for the changes I will note, but I do not wish to explore the political or social aspects of them at this time. Philosophically, the attitude has shifted away from looking for ways to add to the numbers of people served and thus increase the size of an office or department, to merely trying to substantiate a current level of survival. Department heads, agency directors, and committee chairpeople no longer entertain thoughts of adding positions or funds to their offices because they realize the money is probably unavailable or already earmarked for other priorities. At present, large posters in state and federal offices accent the cutbacks in government hiring, resulting in too few people trying to serve an ever-increasing number of clients. Because fewer young and energetic people are being hired for civil service positions, the older, more entrenched and indoctrinated employees remain. This lack of new blood has decreased the potential for new ideas or new challenges within the "system" which helped make it grow once before. Nowadays, rules are followed strictly and new approaches are discouraged, particularly if they require more funding. But perhaps the greatest distinction between current attitudes, and those of years past, lies in the desired outcomes for clients and counselors or social workers. A few years ago employees of the government used to seek the best methods to help people attain economic independence with less attention given to the cost of the services required. It seems today that bureaucratic involvement is limited to a more select clientele and the outcome is often an increased dependence of those clients on the financial benefits available.

Perhaps as times become less austere, the atmosphere and outlook of government agencies and offices will become less stoic and more humane. Until that time, however, each encounter with such bureaucracies must be anticipated with some apprehension as not only are their fewer and fewer civil servants to aid those in need, but there are so many more people now in need of those services.

THE UNEMPLOYMENT OFFICE—INITIAL ENCOUNTER

When the financial reality of having no regular income is ultimately accepted, there remains only one viable solution, outside of a job, for daily existence and that is through either the social welfare system or unemployment benefits. Our government draws a distinction, both philosophically and financially, between these two vehicles, but the first-time recipient often lumps it all together as a handout. Welfare grants are tax-free, but unemployment benefits are indeed taxable. This difference alone should relieve some of the anxiety of getting help through unemployment. Also, welfare grants are derived from government funds obtained through public taxes; unemployment benefits are the result, primarily, of premiums for such insurance paid by employers. All-in-all, these monies are not "charity donations," even if they feel that way to the recipient.

The unemployment office may seem like a cold and grim place when first experienced but through familiarity some of this sullenness tends to disappear. Clearly, it will never be a place of jubilation, but by seeking out the quirks and learning to understand the process it can perhaps become more bearable. If perceptions of what goes on in such an agency are largely the result of media exposure, then the only clarifying statement appropriate to add would be to multiply the negative effects many times to gain a more accurate perception of how things actually are.

For some strange reason, it seems that you are expected to already know what to do when you first go in. Though states and counties and cities differ widely on how services are delivered, there seems to be some unspoken understanding that if a person is applying for unemployment benefits, he or she should already know to get in a particular line, take a particular number, go to a particular office first, or arrive at a particular time of day. Getting over the first feelings of despair and helplessness is turned into a real challenge when confronted with so many unspoken rules and procedures. While more companies are trying to provide some information to their released employees on how, where, and when to file for benefits, this is largely inadequate in the face of such emotional and psychological trauma. For many unemployed, this is probably the first time that assistance has ever been sought, in any form, and a great loss of self-dignity is apparent. To feel forced, financially, to accept that life is going to be so dependent on these other people and their imposing regulations is a very tough pill to swallow. Thoughts and feelings of total disbelief and denial nearly force some people out of the office and back to a more secure place, but somehow they know they have to make it through the experience and then they can retreat to emotional safety. Being reduced to a number on a display board or a statistic in a weekly report is very dehumanizing and to know that it is all happening through no fault of one's own makes things even more uncomfortable.

When the initial shock wears off, a few "facts of life" remain abundantly clear. In exchange for self-respect you are getting an opportunity to let something else reorganize your life with a new set of priorities. The most important thing in your daily existence now becomes the expectation of following rules of the system perfectly or risk losing the only source of financial security during this period. This requires that you learn the policies, procedures, and deadlines of the system very thoroughly. Also, you may gain an otherwise unused ability to sit or stand idly by as you wait your turn to respond to questions from others whose primary interest is in getting you off the unemployment roles. To endure all of this demands that you surrender a certain amount of autonomy over this part of your life. Your aim, above all, during this period should be to exercise as much control over the situation as possible without alienating an entire staff or agency.

RUBBING ELBOWS WITH THE OTHER FAILURES

Not long ago, generalizations about the people who could be found in unemployment offices usually focused on their moral character or their race or their nationality. Most people felt that filing for unemployment benefits was either an easy way to live for lazy people or that the benefits were a lark for actors who were between jobs. How the times have changed! The one common thread in the minds of those who now wait in these offices is that they must all be failures or they wouldn't be here. The feelings of failure, though largely irrational, I could see in the joyless faces of those who surrounded me and in the self-questioning that arose when confronted with the reality of so many others in a similar situation. Is this how my life was going to be from now on? What did I do to deserve this? Those are the kinds of questions you may continue to ask as you wait and watch what is happening around you.

It should become clear that, potentially, there is a strong support system for irrational beliefs and feelings such as these. In the manner in which the bureaucracy functions lies a perpetuating force for individuals to think illogically. A real "Catch-22" exists. If you try to maintain your own self-esteem and individuality, you must deny that you have failed or been, in any way, the cause of this experience. In denying the personal failure or role in the current situation, you must ignore all of the evidence to the contrary. In relationship to other individuals already indoctrinated, you are the illogical or irrational one. If you give in to the dependency and anonymity of the system you would be accepting its irrational beliefs. Hopefully, your own patience and internal controls prevail and you are able to do the things expected of you and return to an otherwise normal existence. But without question there is an emotional tug of war that wages each time you are forced to interact with the bureaucracy.

Other recipients or claimants can also form a large dysfunctional support group that helps to perpetuate nonproductive thoughts and feelings. Many are very angry and hostile people. Their resentment may be directed at everything and everyone remotely associated with them being where they are. For example, politicians are all crooks, they feel; or, their fellow workers set them up to get fired; bosses and/or owners are less than human; and even their own families won't help them! Needless to say, rich people and the government bureaucracies are considered the real criminals in this picture. Maintaining feelings of anger is very easy when thrown into a group such as this.

Another support group for unhealthy feelings is comprised of those individuals who appear to be able to accept all benefits with little or no visible sign of lost pride or dignity. These people sincerely believe that the system owes them a job with the financial benefits of a top executive. Their indignation rises if asked to consider a minimum wage job. But more striking than these characteristics are the unrealistic views of the future. Their aims center around the seemingly short-term need of benefits because of an impending job in another state or with a close relative's business. Their denial of the facts with complete certainty has become a pattern of behavior that seems to lessen the immediate fear of being jobless but in the long run, only serves to prolong and increase the anxiety of being unemployed.

As can be seen, there are ample opportunities to gain support for the anger, hostility, and denial that may be felt during a period of unemployment. Even though these things may seem alien at first, in time they become more and more acceptable as ways to diminish the personal feelings of despair, helplessness, and inadequacy that characterize being unemployed. Perhaps by examining the nature of the actors in this play more closely, some understanding can be gained with which to make better sense of the entire experience.

THE UNEMPLOYMENT CASTE SYSTEM

After a number of visits to the unemployment office and job center, it becomes possible to distinguish a type of caste system that is observed and utilized by both employees and applicants or recipients. It should become clear that such a system serves some very basic needs of these two groups although the classifications actually exist only in the numbers of those who are unemployed. By being able to label one of the unemployed individuals properly, a civil servant can more efficiently deal with that person. Obviously, an experienced applicant does not require as much direction as one coming in for the first time. In recognizing a distinction between the experienced or naive, the system itself lends some credibility to the existence of such differences and thus encourages the applicants to view one another as more or less experienced in the ways of the system. For some of those who are unemployed, perceiving themselves as being an authority in this area is the only semblance of self-esteem that may be observed. For others it only adds to their feelings of degradation and powerlessness. To still others, to be in a position to advise a person similarly out of work is a realistic goal to strive toward. In this sense, the caste system may add some purpose to an otherwise aimless existence.

Group I—First-Time Offenders

In the caste system, the first-time offenders are at the low end of the pecking order. They are treated with disdain by both the system and the other, more experienced unemployed. Being completely ignorant and naive of how and what to do, they are often ignored or rebuffed. These individuals are very easy to distinguish as they generally look completely overwhelmed by what is going on around them. The sheer numbers and amount of time spent waiting in lines boggles the brains of the first-time offenders as they attempt to follow every direction and regulation. They may be seen carrying a host of unrelated files or papers such as W-2 forms of past years' income, insurance forms, letters of recommendation, and others. Also, they may be dressed as though they were having a job interview at any moment. The first-time offenders genuinely believe the system will be their redemption if they do things properly.

The initial experience at the unemployment office may be likened to the judicial system. You may feel as if, in fact, you have committed a crime by becoming unemployed. The "sentence" is in being subjected to the dehumanizing experience of bureaucratic involvement and its negative side effects. The "rehabilitation" is ensured by the fear of remaining involved with either the system or the other members of the caste. Any job that can release you from further experiences such as these would be fine—the sooner the better. If you are not "rehabilitated", you know there is at least a good chance for "parole", which may be obtained by either getting work temporarily or by exhausting the benefits. Learning the ropes is the most important survival skill of this first-time offender.

Group II—Three-Time Losers

The three-time losers are the real pros of the entire system. They have learned the operating procedures of each bureau and can use them to their own best advantage. They are never intimidated or overwhelmed by what is going on around them. These individuals always carry the correct forms, signatures, and copies to a meeting. On one occasion I saw a three-time loser redirect the efforts of a placement counselor to a more advantageous personal position. After getting the address and phone number for a desired temporary job, the applicant was quickly on his way to a day's work—no forms to fill out, no questions to answer! The counselor never knew what happened! If it would appear that a trip may be wasted, this cagey veteran can easily have necessary information obtained over the phone without even leaving the office or losing a place in line. An interesting point that I noticed in talking with and watching these individuals in action was their intimate working knowledge of the requirements for obtaining and retaining benefits, or partial benefits, and their ability to always be released from a job in the proper way to ensure easy requalification. They will never *quit* an uncomfortable job, but they might get fired.

The three-time losers, as a group, are relatively few. They are singled out as models to which others can be compared. The "crime" of the three-time loser is in their inability to plan and take responsibility for their future. A job, to them, is primarily a means to an end, and this is most often an immediate goal rather than a long-term dream such as owning a home. Living as survivors, these individuals are serving a "sentence" comprised of seeking a job, finding and then losing it, and reapplying for unemployment benefits. "Rehabilitation" is unlikely because the system is a friend rather than an enemy of this group so there is no revulsion in dealing with it. "Parole" is the best that the three-time losers can hope for as they go from one job to another.

Group III—Incorrigibles

The incorrigibles represent the smallest group of the caste system. They carry with them the scars from a system that has failed them and that they now hold in total contempt. Regardless of where the blame may actually lie, the incorrigible believes totally and without regret that bureaucracies *owe* them something. In supporting such a position, these individuals are able to justify any action to get the most out of the system. They may refuse any kind of work, at any wage for the most unsupportable reasons.

After once again applying for benefits, one individual told me that he would absolutely refuse to work again until his twenty-six weeks of benefits had expired. After all, the system *owed* him that money! He also felt very strongly that the money obtained from unemployment should not be taxable because he and his wife may have to pay the government back. An unspoken belief of the incorrigible is that benefits should be, at minimum, equal to the gross pay for a minimum-wage job of forty hours a week, and be available for as long as it takes to find another comparable job!

To achieve their ends, these individuals will rationalize any form of behavior as acceptable in order to get what they see as rightfully owed to them. Nothing is sacred, short of their own motives, to obtain more than anyone else has ever gotten before them. Adding dependents to welfare reports, misusing food stamps, inventing new names with new social security numbers are all acceptable lines of action for the incorrigible. Needless to say, undeclared income is a very proper way of increasing the amount of cash without decreasing a benefit check and this is standard operating procedure for this group. By being involved with as many different agencies and departments as possible at once, it may become very easy to set up smokescreens and develop diversions in order to get more from each one. Creating internal conflict between agencies is a common method used to enhance the probability that services might be duplicated.

The "crime" of incorrigibles is in their way of life that seems to them to be so totally acceptable. With few moral principles, they have been "sentenced" to a life of conflict, threat, and manipulation from both within and outside the system. There is little or no hope for "rehabilitation" because they feel no need for it.

I have outlined and described the existence of three distinct types of individuals who may be encountered in many of the social service agencies but more specifically in an unemployment office. While the second and third groups probably exist in relatively small numbers, they should be recognized as examples of what can happen to people who are forced into such a jobless state. In fact, the vast numbers of unemployed are most likely indicative of group one or only slightly more experienced than that. But because of a very stressful situation the influence of the three-time losers or incorrigibles on this larger group can become a real danger. I feel that only by continuing to compare personal beliefs and values to these kinds of examples, is a person able to maintain a relatively stable course throughout the ordeal of unemployment.

LEARNING THE SYSTEM

After a few episodes of being in the wrong place at the wrong time, it may be discovered there are some things that can be done to make life a little more comfortable when dealing with the system. Because procedures are handled differently from place to place, the specific items listed may not apply across the board but the motives should be similar. Keeping in mind that the experienced applicants will not willingly share their own survival techniques, you will probably have to observe as much as possible before coming up with your own best efforts. As starting points, the following observations may be very appropriate.

The Bad, Worse, and Worst Days

With deadlines to meet and crowds to contend with, unemployment offices are forced to schedule and regiment as much activity as possible. Experienced claimants discover that the particular pattern of any office or bureau can be broken down. Based on this pattern a determination is made as to which is the best day to go to the office for services. Without mistake, there are days that are better for some things and worse for others.

For instance, Monday, Tuesday, and Wednesday are absolutely the worst days to go to the unemployment office or job service center. Admittedly you may have to find this out the hard way, but once learned, you will be able to get more done and waste less time. There are some very understandable reasons why these days are worse than Thursday or Friday. To begin with, because of the nature of payrolls and pink-slips, many people find themselves unemployed on a Friday after work or a Monday morning just before a new week starts. Obviously, there will be a rush to the unemployment office by those who are inexperienced in joblessness, and this begins on Monday and may last through Tuesday if the week before has claimed many casualties. Basically, the numbers swell because the inexperienced just don't know any better and they have no appreciation for the events yet to come, so they flock in to register and wait in long lines or tightly filled rooms.

To the knowledgeable recipient, these first three days represent a very different picture than that for the new applicant. If any discrepancies with forms, signatures, or computer reporting have occurred, they must be cleared up quickly to ensure that there is little or no break in the benefits. Generally, these must be taken care of by Wednesday to have any chance of either resuming benefits or continuing them uninterrupted. It is also very apparent that civil service employees are critically aware of the early-week push as they facilitate or inhibit quick progression of people through the process. If it appears there is the potential for some game-playing here, it is an accurate perception. While the applicants are very serious about what they are trying to do and they usually wish to get it done quickly and leave, the entire program can be held up for a staff conversation about a legal point, a telephone call from home or a friend, or just about anything else imaginable. In this show, the system orchestrates all of the steps and calls all of the shots while the players simply react to what is happening. During these three days, the goals of the applicants are generally consistent. Most want to do the necessary paperwork or clear up any discrepancies and get out to try and find work. These goals, however, seem to be at odds with those of the system. At times they may demand some new piece of information or another appointment of an applicant. Another goal may be to just answer the internal needs of the system for order and deliberation.

Thursdays are better than the first three days of the week to go into the office for anything, but they still are not very good. By Thursday all of the critical questions and items have been taken care of and the most experienced people know to wait for Friday, which is the best day to go in anyway. The crowds of people on the fourth day are made up primarily of those who were not seen on Wednesday because time ran out. These individuals are showing the first signs of learning the system as they make the connection that the first ones in are the first ones out, usually. As they continue the relationship with the unemployment office, this piece of information proves to be invaluable.

Also arriving on Thursday are a throng of new applicants who may be processed as a group because their needs are all the same initially. Though this does not usually mean having to wait until they have completed their indoctrination to be seen, it does lessen the number of civil servants who are available to work with others who need help. The atmosphere in the unemployment office starts to relax on Thursday as the biggest push of people is over and the weekend is in sight.

The optimum day to go in for services is Friday. Because Friday will be the last day of work for many who are being fired or laid off, it is important to get into the unemployment office or job center before this new group discovers its loss and converges on Monday. From a more practical standpoint, there are fewer people to contend with on Friday because of some less related reasons. First, as the experience of unemployment and involvement with government agencies goes on, there is a growing revulsion for it. In order to not get a weekend off to a bad start, many people simply stay away from the office until they absolutely have to go in. People such as these take three-day weekends to collect the energy to go in on Monday. Others simply know that not a great deal can be done to rush an unemployment check if there has been some bureaucratic or computer foul-up and to still others, procrastination wins out as they oversleep or just put off going in until another time. In terms of the process itself, even if an individual is required to report to the unemployment office or job service center on a Friday there is usually a seven-day period in which to come in. In such a case, there should never be a deadline on a Friday if a person simply schedules around it.

Unfortunately, there are two drawbacks to waiting until Friday. First, others have discovered the functional reality of the system, and they, too, choose Friday to go into the office. Also, as sheer numbers of those filing for unemployment remain high, Friday will probably blend in with the rest of the week as a poor time to go in. Second, the unemployment office employees recognize the diminished numbers and tend to relax a little more. The net result is that, though there may be fewer people to see, they are not seen in any less time than normal. On Monday, two hundred people may be attended to in a working day; on Friday, one hundred will take just as long.

Times to Go In

Basically, there is not a good or best time of the day to try to get into the unemployment office. Some times may be better than others, but those are quickly discovered by everyone so there is generally a crowd of people at every seemingly opportune moment. However, there are a few time periods that may entail the least amount of wasted time. By getting to the office very early, the chances are good that you can get in and out fairly quickly. This usually means that you have to get there thirty or forty minutes before it opens, but once inside you are seen right away. It quickly becomes apparent that others feel the same as you do about going in early, so you have to determine a point of diminishing return for your waiting. I found this to be about forty-five minutes and I would not go any earlier. After all, there was little difference between waiting inside for an hour or ninety minutes where it might be warm and waiting outside for an hour where the weather might be very unappealing. Regardless of which was actually the most efficient, I learned to always take some reading material because I was in for a long wait.

The alternative to arriving early is to go in an hour before the office closes. Arriving late in the day guarantees that you will not have to wait longer than 60 minutes, but you do risk not being seen at all. Keeping in mind that Fridays are usually the slowest anyway, the afternoon timing may be most productive. Also, because some offices arbitrarily stop seeing clients an hour before they actually close, it is occasionally possible to get something easy or simple taken care of without waiting at all.

Overall, as previously stated, there is not a good or best time to ever go into these offices. If certain business must be taken care of at an exact time or on a particular day, there may be no alternative as to when you must go in. Families with infants or children to get off to school must contend with these times before even considering when to go to the unemployment office. Job interviews are paramount so they must be given priority over other things. One point to keep in mind is that the bureaucracy will go on with or without the unemployed people it tries to serve so there is little incentive for flexibility or compassion on the part of the system. Sometimes the best way to get things done is to do the waiting, or pay the dues, and then move on to more productive activites.

DEALING WITH THE SYSTEM

As is the case with almost any public or private agency or bureau, if there are rules, regulations, or procedures to follow, there are certainly exceptions for each of them. In learning to contend with the government bureaucracies, I was able to observe some very interesting techniques used by others to most effectively gain what they needed. I am sure these particular examples cannot be applied to all unemployment offices but the point behind each is to somehow regain some sense of dignity, even if nothing material is won in the process. At least some resistance to the demoralizing and demeaning process itself is shown, and that alone is reason enough to try some things. I should caution that nothing of financial or legal consideration should be toyed with as this could result in losing benefits or having to repay amounts of money along with interest later on. It is not uncommon to feel that an adversarial relationship exists between applicants and the civil servants particularly because only one is being paid for the time being spent together. Therefore, if a way can be managed to lessen the time required to complete forms or interviews, so much the better for all concerned.

One day I observed a seasoned veteran of the unemployment war implement what I call the "take-a-number-but-don't-wait approach." Upon entering the office, he quickly received a number that determined in what order he would be seen. At this point, however, he did not move away to take a seat or to get in a line. He remained at the counter until one of the employees asked what he needed. With that he rapidly explained his entire problem and waited for a response. When asked if he had a number, he quickly replied "yes" and repeated his wishes. Before service was rendered, however, he was asked to show his number. At this, he became very disheartened and walked away to take his place with the rest of us. This approach sometimes works and even if it doesn't, you only have to get in line and wait as you would have anyway.

I witnessed a similar tactic one morning that I call the "take-a-number-see-you-later-routine." Upon entering the unemployment office, three plant workers quickly got their numbers. By noting what number was being served and how many numbers came before theirs, they were able to make a fair estimate as to how long it would be before they would be seen. They based their estimate on a rate of fifteen minutes per number and based from observations I felt that was fairly close. At any rate, they left only to return some time later just in time to be seen. A word of caution here too is in order, however. No one will warn you if you are about to be called, even if you are only outside smoking a cigarette. Each number that is skipped over means that someone else is seen that much sooner.

Other survival techniques used or observed include a redefinition of certain English words. A word such as "volunteer" may mean that something is done freely and with no expectation of financial gain. Therefore, money received for "volunteer" work might not be claimed as wages, which would reduce a weekly benefit amount. *Severance Pay* might be interpreted as money given to help with private placement bureau fees, travel expenses to interviews or other job-seeking costs, but it should not be used to delay the receipt of benefits. Last, *sick pay* is money a person received for staying well; therefore, it should not delay the receipt of unemployment benefits because it is clearly not a form of wages.

Errors

Because the bureaucracy tends to be so large and cumbersome, you may find through experience that you can anticipate errors being made in the overall process as a result of either computer mistakes or human foul-ups. The interesting aspect of this, however, is that the employees working in the offices also expect such errors and generally encourage people to take the course of least resistance when trying to correct any of them. In a particular case, two such incidents occurred. Upon starting to receive benefits a number of weeks too soon, an individual inquired as to what to do with the money. The problem was solved when the person was told to *always* keep the money because the computer would certainly go haywire if a check were returned uncashed. Also, there appeared to be little doubt that the computer would ultimately catch the error and somehow correct it. With that in mind, the individual continued to deposit the checks for another twelve weeks. The individual did, however, receive a computer letter demanding the full remittance of three weeks benefits or they would be penalized and all future payments forfeited. Ironically, that letter came from the same office on the same day as another benefit check.

After receipt of such a letter the individual was impelled to go back into the unemployment office to make arrangements for repayment. A plan was settled upon that would have the computer subtract one-half of the total benefit each week for a six week period, after which time the entire amount due would be repaid. The first repayment subtraction went very well, but when the second deduction was being made, a statement of account was sent showing the amount which was still owed was far greater than the total amount which was ever received! The computer goofed again. If allowed to progress, this person would have owed the Department of Labor several thousand dollars in a very short time. Once again, a return visit to the unemployment office was made to try and straighten matters out.

Never Telephone

If there is any question as to why the telephone is never used to get such matters cleared up, all I can say is good luck. After a number of very heated conversations and being hung-up on, one individual learned that the telephone was used for anything but conducting business with the unemployment office. Because of the increased number of applicants and a government freeze on hiring, the workloads are too overwhelming for employees to spend time helping someone over the phone. Although there may be ample time to make social dates or conduct personal matters, this should not be construed to mean that any productive business can be done over the phone. The logic for such a policy is based upon the notion that during the day there are too many clients to see to answer questions on the phone, and after the clients have been served, there is too much paperwork to be completed for anyone to talk on the phone or answer a question. All of this only adds to the frustration and anger so evident during this period, but it seems there is little that can rationally be done other than to endure it and move on.

SHORTCOMINGS OF THE SYSTEM

As it presently exists, there are some major shortcomings of such a system. The first and foremost drawback is that the system encourages otherwise honest people to, at best, bend or, at worst, break the rules. The financial pressures of being jobless and the emotional pressures of hopelessness and despair can push people to deny that money was earned from a part-time job. People may also refuse suitable work because it will not pay as much as their unemployment benefit. In both cases the actions are improper, but each occurs too often to accurately determine. In one instance, I inquired about what to do if I earned some money from a part-time job. I was told to get paid in cash and not declare it. This advice came from one of the employment counselors! Though I never worked part-time, I might have been hard pressed not to consider the advice even though I was aware it was against the rules.

A more pervasive shortcoming of the system lies in the psychological dependence it creates. When compared to classical forms of brainwashing, the experiences of the unemployed are very similar. Initial encounters tend to strip away much of the self-esteem and self-respect a person may have. Being so vulnerable, you are then forced to contend with incredible financial and personal pressures while being subjected to the dehumanizing experience of joblessness. This being the case quite often, unemployment benefits become the primary focus for major life reorganization. The system provides money, it provides short-term security, and it may provide for other needs as well. In some instances, the system actually provides work. Overall, this creates a tremendous feeling of dependence and certainly lessens the likelihood for any healthy risk-taking or venturing to occur on the part of jobless individuals.

Finally, in such a system, people are sometimes forced to get fired rather than resign a nonproductive job. Because benefits are not quickly forthcoming if just cause cannot be shown for being unemployed, an individual is faced with choosing between the two unpleasant alternatives of not receiving benefits or having a major blemish on an otherwise very respectable work history.

REDEMPTIONS OF THE SYSTEM

The previous points accent some negative aspects of both the bureaucracy and the individuals who are involved with it. There are, however, some very important redeeming qualities of civil servants and the agencies they represent.

Though the unemployment office, or what it may represent psychologically, is not the ultimate in pleasure it does serve a most needed function. Without doubt, the benefits provide many millions of jobless individuals the only available source of any financial security. Whether 26 or even 32 weeks of payments are enough to weather such a storm remains to be seen, although it appears it may be. Second, the unemployment office or job service center provides viable employment leads to a sector of the population that would otherwise go unserved. During the best of economic times these agencies have never provided a great deal for highly educated professionals, but certain states, cities, or locales are now attempting to help even this group through special programs and placement practices.

For those who work in these agencies, the jobs at times must seem thankless and pessimistic. Civil servants are forced to function under awkward rules, regulations, and procedures when they, too, may see the inefficiency of it all. While I have had my interactions with both the "Scrooges" and the "Nurse Ratchit" types, in the main, most of the counselors, case workers, and employees have been as helpful as possible.

Given the circumstances of joblessness and insecurity, the unemployed individual is much like a cornered animal. He or she must fight for existence against all odds. Anything within striking distance will usually be forced to endure his or her wrath. Only by seeing the bureaucracy with its imperfections and flaws, as well as its strengths, can you begin to move through this experience with as little emotional damage as possible.

chapter five

Surveying the Damage

Before ever starting to consider the actual financial disorientation incurred by becoming unemployed, you must first try to assess the psychological and emotional trauma of the event. Even if you are able to anticipate many of the reactions to your unemployed status from friends and family, you may be less prepared to deal with some of the very marked changes that occur within you.

I have long known that during periods of personal difficulty or reorganization, the most important stabilizing factors, in any psychological sense, are perceptions a person may have about him or herself. These concepts form over a long period of time and are the result of experiences and interactions with an individual's total world in general and with a group of significant people in particular. For most people such a group of significant others is comprised of parents, siblings, husbands or wives, teachers or counselors, and perhaps a few close friends. Because this is such a small group, the perceptions, once formed, are relatively stable and may be very resistant to change. As a person grows older, this circle of influence becomes even smaller as parents may die or, ultimately, a spouse and one's close friends begin to leave the world. Therefore, how a person views him or herself as a youngster may ultimately have a great influence upon how he or she sees him or herself while growing up, leaving home, choosing a vocation, marrying, becoming a parent, and so on. These perceptions can be as impacted by failure, personal loss or professional setback, as by success, interpersonal rewards, or other typically positive life experiences.

Even for those individuals whose early life history was accented by caring and concerned parents who demonstrated love and encouraged healthy growth, the crisis of unemployment may be a period of deep self-doubt and of feeling defeated. Generally positive and meaningful life experiences may not prevent the alienated or fragmented feelings that result from an extended period of forced idleness. For many individuals who have not experienced a personally rewarding or emotionally stable life, unemployment can be a crucial blow to an already fragile ego and self-concept. These people often take some very disastrous means to cope with their seemingly unfriendly and uncaring world. Increasing instances of alcohol and/or drug abuse, spouse or child battering, criminal behavior, and even suicide all point to the destructive effects of being unemployed for long periods of time. With little feeling of hope or power to change a dismal situation, life can become a very desperate struggle just to survive.

After losing a job, you may notice a number of rapid and unhealthy changes that take place within you and in your daily life. One such person I met had always felt proud of his ability to use personal skills and qualities effectively to help other people achieve both long and short-term goals. He felt a strong sense of purpose in what he did and experienced a great deal of personal satisfaction in helping others obtain their desired ends. Most certainly, a fair salary for a job well done was also rewarding, but to him this was like icing on the cake. When he realized that there would no longer be an opportunity to help the customers and colleagues whom he had worked with for so many years, he suddenly felt very empty. Much as a teacher who can no longer enter the daily arena of the classroom and use the skills so painstakingly attained, he too had lost his field of activity and along with it, all sense of meaning and purpose. A teacher derives a tremendous sense of fulfillment from helping students to grow and prosper. When this potential is taken away, there is no longer a means of feeling the same personal satisfaction for a job well done.

Besides the empty feeling of purposelessness, he experienced too, the loss of an ability to actually see any tangible benefits of his actions. While he worked at his job, he could observe both the financial and personal benefits of being very good at what he did. As sales increased, the company prospered and grew. Because this growth never occurred before, he felt responsible for much of it and that was very gratifying. Equally as rewarding was the ability to maintain so many genuinely pleased customers. These kinds of people provided a rich source of positive feedback, which certainly fostered feelings of personal success. Upon being released from his job, he felt that he had lost all potential for ever seeing any results of doing a good job. He could no longer take pride in either maintaining or increasing sales. On the contrary, upon termination he was made to feel personally responsible for sales not made or profits not realized. Just as a skilled craftsperson will grow to question his or her own ability to ply a personal trade if unable to practice it, he began to question his own personal abilities and qualities as an effective employee.

Feelings of adequacy are fostered not only by the financial results obtained for the company as a result of doing an effective job, but also by the attainment or nearing of more personal goals. To some, these less concrete aspects are every bit as important as the more financial or profit-centered ones.

Regardless of company gains from their efforts, people feel a tremendous sense of reward and accomplishment when personal goals or levels are reached. For instance, I always felt challenged to make sales without the use of deception, or fast talk, although practiced by others around me. To establish a level of trust with a customer and then fulfill that expectation was my measure of success. I had established my own standards for judging success and they included the interaction of business skills with personal values and beliefs to attain desired financial outcomes. When I became unemployed, I lost the vehicle to test new limits and abilities. When a professional athlete is cut from a team and can no longer push him or herself to the ends of physical ability, he or she may lose that source of personal affirmation. The athlete may begin to question not only the current skill level, but actually wonder if he or she was ever any good. Similar questions went through my mind as they have no doubt entered the thoughts of millions of others who have become unemployed. I wondered if, in fact, I was ever really skilled at what I did. More important, I questioned the beliefs I had about loyalty, honesty, and hard work.

CHANGE IN VALUES

One of the immediate reactions to the sudden loss of a job is to make a silent promise that you will *never* again be in such a personally vulnerable position. Although this is, I feel, a move toward future safety, you must also realize that it may be the beginning of some doubting of long-held beliefs and values. To attain the goal of personal security, you may become willing to do whatever might be necessary. Beliefs in honesty and fair play sometimes become relegated to secondary importance behind another stated purpose.

Compromising one's values during a period such as this can take place almost without knowing it. Upon occasion you may find yourself saying things and acting in ways that only weeks before would have been totally alien to you. At this time in life, thoughts are characterized by self-doubt and recrimination as you wonder what you are turning into and why you are letting yourself change. An overwhelming anxiety about the future coupled with a need to be reemployed, and thus useful again, result in the controlling of interaction and conversation with potential employers as well as the distortion of skills, abilities, and experiences. To a person who values truth, openness, and honesty, these kinds of actions are very hard to accept. During an interview, one individual told me that when asked what or where he wanted to be in five years, he became very evasive and self-conscious. Having disclosed those dreams to a previous employer and ultimately having been released, he had no desire to have the same thing happen again. Needless to say, the result of such behavior can be both emotionally painful for an employee and certainly potentially harmful for an employer who may believe what he or she is being told. As weeks and even months pass without employment, the tendency to become more protective increases and an active and conscious effort must be made to lessen this need. If allowed to continue, this tendency can result in a vicious circle of unhealthy behavior and a complete loss of self-respect. You must realize that by being so evasive in responses, you actually diminish the strong qualities of openness and honesty. In doing this, you fail to demonstrate two great assets. With such a competitive job market as now exists, everyone needs to put his or her best foot forward—particularly at an interview. The net result of a less-than-the-best interview is often a certain elimination from consideration as an employee. As this occurs, it tends to reinforce any inadequate feelings already existing and makes a person even more protective and less open. Thus, the circle is complete.

Another traditional value that may begin to disintegrate is a natural respect for other people. As one individual remained unemployed for a longer and longer period, she could feel a change in the way she viewed others who were either applying for the same job or who had been colleagues and were still working. People who are similarly unemployed seem to become enemies because you fear that they might possibly be better qualified or perhaps know someone in a position to influence the decision on who to hire. Representing such a threat, you may become suspicious of their abilities and experiences. In terms of any personal dignity, you may feel that such a group cannot be trusted and thus deserves little respect. Such paranoia is unfounded and if allowed to intensify can become the sole source of thoughts and actions toward others in the same boat as you.

Without some guideposts or markers to use as comparisons, like the classes of unemployed mentioned in the previous chapter, behaviors such as lying, deception, or distrust may become commonplace where they were once nonexistent. But there are other equally unhealthy changes that can also occur such as the development of an irrational need for money or an uncompromising drive for financial security. Granted, if economic pressures of outstanding debts, family support or living expenses are great, the need for money may appear all consuming. However, if financial pressures had previously produced only minimal employment concerns, this shift in importance can cause some very distinct changes in a person's behavior and beliefs. One individual I encountered who had recently lost his job, was evidently in a process of becoming overwhelmed with the need to make money. Every ounce of energy he expended was directed toward getting a few more dollars. The price he was paying for such a change was, I felt, too dear. He gave up the companionship of his wife and family in his quest for financial independence. His personal and social life suffered immeasurably as his children felt alienated by his change in behavior and his friends were able to interact with him on only one subject—money, or how to get more of it. If he ever realizes absolute financial security, I am not sure he will still want it when he discovers the price he has paid.

Perhaps, the primary redeeming change in any beliefs or values that I have personally experienced and noticed in others is a movement toward greater independence or self-reliance. Once you recognize that you do not want to be so vulnerable to such emotional trauma again, you may begin to explore ways to prevent it from recurring. Ironically, your ability to provide total financial security may be no greater than before, but, the ability to contend with a deep personal loss is much greater than before becoming unemployed. This sense of psychological strength can be very reassuring and may ultimately be the primary basis of any positive outcomes of losing a job.

INDIRECT CAUSES OF CHANGE

As previously described, there are some basic causes for the changes in how a person views him or herself during a period of unemployment. The perceptions gained and nurtured from youthful experiences with parents and friends are brought into question and strongly challenged. Also, values once held dear are closely scrutinized as feelings of inadequacy and powerlessness result in behaviors of distrust for others and conflict with friends or family members.

But other influences are also at work during this period and these, too, help to bring about changes in how a person may view his or her own worth and ability. After losing her job, one person found that former colleagues were reluctant and even resistant to spending leisure time with her. Aside from the personal loss of their friendship which was felt, she was being treated like an exiled leper. Some mutual acquaintances have since let her know that those former coworkers were afraid they would not feel comfortable in her presence because they were certain she would be vindictive, hostile or, very angry about being released. True or not, the result is that she does not have the relationship with these people that she had enjoyed just a brief time ago. In this instance, losing a job meant losing friends also.

As one sales executive reflected on some of the more obvious causes of being released, he could see that his own salary level was a major contributing factor to the decision to let him go. No longer having to pay his salary was one way to markedly reduce the company's overhead very quickly. Strange as it seemed, the success he had enjoyed through the years helped put him in a position of being without the job he did so well. I have now come to realize that a salary certainly plays a major role in how a person may view his or her personal worth as an employee and as a citizen. If a salary is low, there is a tendency to dicount the importance of the job to the company and its customers. Conversely, if the salary is high, an inflated or distorted view may occur. In either case, the salary level itself is probably less an indication of a job's relative importance to a company as it is of that company's ability to pay it to anyone who may hold the job. Perhaps this can explain why there appear to be an abundance of both underpaid secretaries and overpaid managers.

One last indirect cause of personal changes that I have observed seemed to be a boredom felt during the prolonged period of forced idleness. Immediately after losing a job, there are an endless number of things to do. Register with the unemployment office or other bureaus, prepare résumés or applications, contact known employers, and many other less significant activities fill the waking hours of each day. As time wears on, however, the activities lessen and more time is spent being inactive than active. The lack of meaningful things to do or involvement with other people can set into motion another vicious circle of behavior. Because of being unemployed and unable to find another job quickly, you may feel depressed. Feeling depressed about having nothing to do, you do not feel like initiating new inquiries. As a result, there are fewer chances of actually getting work that creates even more idle time and greater depression. With this circle complete, you may find yourself doubting your own abilities and worth more often, and ultimately may be forced to take strong action to change the scenario. This action usually takes the form of making yourself talk to others, exercising out of doors, or scheduling meetings with friends for lunch or just conversation. I believe that the specific types of actions chosen to alter this vicious circle of behavior are less important than the fact that an effort is consciously being made to change what is happening. By redirecting energies into more personally rewarding activities, you are able to break the circle and prevent further negative effects.

LOSS OF SECURITY

Perhaps the single most devastating and long-term negative effect of losing a job is the almost instantaneous disappearance of any sense of permanent security. Because so much of an individual's belief about overall security (personal and interpersonal, financial, and vocational) is derived in some form through employment, the immediate impact is felt in all of these areas when a job is lost.

In personal and interpersonal relationships, the impact is evident. After losing a job, you can see a marked change in the ways some friends approach you because they are unsure of how to interact with you. It seems you are a living reminder of what might possibly happen to them. While your own family may be very supportive through this period, these relationships too are not without strain and conflict. I have known individuals who have lost husbands or wives through divorce or separation. These kinds of events are confirmations of a failing life and social alienation. Friends and family members alike move away or become less concerned about the unemployed, thus destroying feelings of belongingness or camaraderie. The resulting loss of personal security, of feeling wanted and needed, is one not replaced with a job alone. This is an example of a long-term human loss, which in many instances is the net result of a short-term business gain.

The need to reestablish a feeling of financial security can become an overwhelming factor in determining how you use your time and energy as well as how any remaining income from a spouse will be used. Once becoming unemployed, you are saddled with a deep doubt that real financial security is even possible. With no regular income and an uncertain future, you realize that your health must remain good until you have medical insurance again. Similarly, automobile driving must become even more careful as the auto insurance must be changed, if not cancelled. You may consider the real possibility of converting the cash value of life insurance policies in order to use the money for other necessities. A job, even a relatively low-paying one, provides an ability to budget for premiums like these. With a regular paycheck, people seldom worry about paying insurance premiums on such policies. While unemployed, what could happen in the event of a serious accident or even a death becomes a major worry. It occurs to me now that there are probably vast numbers of unemployed who are driving with little or no auto insurance, others who have dropped life insurance plans, and still others who may be inadequately insured in other ways. Without a job, these policies are luxuries that become very expendable.

In terms of personal savings, or "nest eggs," unless very sizeable, these are quickly exhausted. Even the savings of older parents or younger children may be called upon to meet the financial burden brought on by prolonged unemployment. Some people who had been able to accumulate a meager savings before losing their job, at least, felt there was something to fall back on. Many others I have spoken with were never able to do this and so when they suddenly lost their job, they were thrown into a series of radical financial adjustments such as selling a car, a house, or other belongings. One person was forced to arrange the relinquishing of a child to a previous spouse because she had no money for the child's food, clothing, and other daily living necessities.

Underlying the social and financial changes experienced is the long-term loss of any real job security. Personally, you may feel somehow misled into believing that if you performed well and maintained your value to a company you would always have a place to work. Realizing that this is not true, you may now come to question if it will ever even be probable. I found through a period of trying to sort out why I was in a jobless position, that, though unrelated, I probably had placed too much dependence for social and financial security on being employed. I have become more self-reliant now for personally fostering friendships or closer relationships with my family. Money earned from working is a means to provide for living necessities, and extras when possible, but as a basis for total financial security, wages are no longer the only means to consider. If job security is a myth, believing in it will only heighten my chances of facing similar financial difficulties in the future. Therefore, I will try to find other ways of assuring a feeling of overall security in years to come.

PERSONAL LOSSES

During the early period of unemployment, one of the most difficult personal adjustments to make is in not seeing or talking to some people who have been a part of a daily routine for many years. For me this meant that at least six individuals would most likely be totally out of my life for a long time, if not forever. Because starting and building very close friendships takes a great deal of time and energy, this adjustment is not an easy one. At times you may want to scream out that you do not care if you were let go at all. You may just want to talk to someone again or ask how his or her life is going, or perhaps share feelings about things. This, however, is a fantasy. The price for embarking on such a close personal *and* professional relationship must be paid when one of the people is let go. If a dollar amount could be applied to this, I am certain it would be very great. I suspect, too, that many have paid such a price.

Long periods of idle time or aimless activities can result in a very fragmented and disorganized life. To be so active, both mentally and physically, one moment and in the next instant not have anything to do is a difficult transition. One friend I spoke with felt as if she were searching for some purpose or meaning in life and were incapable of finding it. Though she knew she might sink in this emotional quicksand, at times she felt powerless to stop it. Because of these experiences, some changes have taken place within her that resulted in a much more cautious and controlled lifestyle. The loyalty toward friends that she prided herself upon before being let go has changed and means something different to her now. The openness to trusting the intent and purpose of other people's actions is now cautious. She needs evidence of a person's good intentions more so now than ever before in her life. Though she still feels that she is very honest and forthright, she realizes that she does not disclose inner thoughts and feelings to others as openly or freely as she once did. Last, because of the changes she has gone through, she knows that her ability to make positive and healthy choices about events in her life is not as strong as before this crisis. Her primary hope is for these new characteristics to recede and to ultimately be and feel the way she once did. But for the present, she knows that she, like many others in similar positions, must maintain her emotional and psychological defenses in order to reorganize life into a safer and more meaningful existence.

EMOTIONAL SCARS

If the actual truth were known, the common denominator for all unemployed individuals is anger. Even if this anger is diminished, the inescapable truth is that it exists in all who are let go. Potentially anger represents the most destructive emotion. If the anger is totally depressed for too long, it can have serious effects on an individual's own mental health. Therefore, any attempt to express and accept these feelings is the initial step in coping with them. Interestingly for some, there is a feeling that they have passed through this period of anger and are handling life quite well. Such was the case of one person who maintained his apparent coping ability until some weeks later when he was asked about his "job" by someone who was unaware he was unemployed. In a matter of seconds he could hear his voice crack and feel his heart pound in his chest as he had to fight to hold down an intense urge to lash out. After the experience, he realized that he had not handled these feelings very well and more work on them was in order. During the first few weeks after my release I found myself being very defensive about the reasons for my firing. My wife expressed her anger and frustration and somehow I always felt a need to defend my former employer. I know now that the healthy thing for me to do would have been to agree with her, add my own feelings and move on. Similar behavior on my part was shown when close friends also expressed their anger. Again, I should have agreed with them and moved on to another topic.

As previously mentioned, a real pitfall in maintaining a healthy outlook on life during this period is the fact that there are so many other unemployed individuals who are very angry and are quite willing to share this feeling with you. Frequently, it requires little or no coaxing to get these people to start ranting or raving about their former employer, co-workers, or the world in general. At a party one evening, I spoke with an old friend I had not seen for some time. As the conversation progressed and I informed him of my being let go from my job, he became increasingly upset and angry. After a period spent venting his feelings, I asked why he was so upset. To this he replied that he, too, was laid off and he felt the decision was cruel, arbitrary, and discriminatory. Obviously, if I kept feeding such a conversation with my own fuel, we could have both become mired in the mud of futility. I chose to redirect the conversation to what might be done about getting reemployed or retrained. This, tactic, I quickly found, was much more productive and less pessimistic.

The dangers of repressing anger lie first in the risk of ultimately becoming very depressed. Second, in needing to control so strong a feeling as anger, other feelings may become depressed along with it. The results of this second point can be seen in less risk-taking or in a diminished capacity to appreciate happy events of life. By taking fewer chances when disclosing dreams and hopes, you keep them safe from the possibility of others being insensitive about them or of being too personally disappointed if they are unfulfilled. Although this tactic provides protection to some degree, you also experience less joy in their attainment. During job interviews you may become preoccupied with saying things or acting in ways you may think the other person is seeking. Because of this, you disclose less of your true self and, in effect, do not really demonstrate strengths and abilities. You are being safe, but you are not helping yourself in the long run.

The need for self-defense and protection from others severely limits the ability to trust or rely on people unless you know them very well. You may begin to believe that others will only let you down and this reinforces the need to become even more self-reliant. This tends only to insulate you from friends even more, but more important, it creates a self-fulfilling prophecy. As you become convinced that very few people can be depended upon to behave the way they should, you look for evidence to support this. The old cliché that "if you walk around with a hammer in your hand long enough, everything starts to look like a nail" applies in this circumstance after losing a job. When you make an appointment with someone and he or she is late or has to cancel, it only serves to confirm the perception that that person should not have been trusted in the first place. This kind of irrational belief does little to foster friendship or closeness with people.

When socializing with others, some unemployed people have less tendency to offer suggestions, help, or even interact. So much emotional energy is being used to try and maintain some organization and meaning in life that there may be little desire to share these thoughts and feelings with other people. Just trying to relax or redirect your own thinking becomes very difficult. This, in part, is the result of two factors. First, when talking to family members or close friends, the topic invariably turns to employment, or an apparent lack of it. Though you may appreciate their genuine concern, you are in no position to talk of abundant job offerings or potential openings. There seems to be little to say of a very positive nature. The second factor is of finances. Because you may be providing very little if anything to the family income, you may feel guilty if money is used frivolously or with little purpose. Before losing a job, a cold glass of beer after a friendly racquetball match is something to be enjoyed. After losing the job, however, this type of activity is severely limited, if not eliminated completely. It may seem that all of the things in life that could help you relax and forget the immediate pressures are financially unavailable. Those things that can do the most to help, are the very things you are forced to stop doing because they cost money. Each time that you noticed another aspect of your life being forcibly altered by being unemployed, you may feel another piece of your world being taken away. The lifestyle you once knew becomes more constricted as the weeks of unemployment pass.

SATISFYING NEEDS

If the need for food and shelter are minimally being met during a crisis such as this, then an individual is able to attempt to satisfy higher level needs such as love, self-esteem, and belongingness. When financial pressures become greater and greater however, the primary needs become the major purpose of life. The higher needs for love and acceptance do not disappear. They are either ignored or satisfied in different ways.

After an extended period of being unemployed, you stop taking some things for granted that may previously have been almost second nature. From a spouse, you may need to actually hear his or her expression of love for you. You may need concrete evidence that his or her feelings for you have not lessened because you are out of work. Even changes in sexual behavior are potential hints of a change in his or her perception of you. These needs, when irrational or largely out of focus, can be very harmful. The slightest alteration in previous habits might be interpreted as either pity or a loss of respect.

From your friends, you may also demand and need more obvious signs of acceptance. If they stop to visit, they have to stay a long time or they are just stopping to be nice. If you visited the same friends, however, it would only be brief so the appearance would be given that you are so busy you could not stay very long. In either instance, false pictures are given or perceived and the end result is a diminished feeling of self-respect.

To maintain previously held beliefs about yourself, it may become necessary to focus attention on the facts that you are genuinely loved by your family and cared about by your close friends. In recognizing and accepting these two things, the negative effects of unemployment can just become a little easier to contend with.

A number of individuals I observed and spoke with who were out of work displayed a marked change in their approach to physical activities during the period of unemployment. One, who was a relatively passive person and had engaged in recreational sports primarily for the fun of them, became very competitive and critical of both his own performance and that of his opponents. It appeared that he was trying to use the competition of sports to elevate his own lowered self-concept and he did it by either winning outright or by demeaning the play of others.

Another person I spoke with decided to take up a total fitness program of jogging and weight training. By enhancing her own physical appearance and thus easing, somewhat, her overall feelings of inadequacy, she was able to also cope with being unemployed a little more effectively. For others, the physical activities seemed good but never really released the tensions they felt or eased their own self-doubt. The most positive effect of exercise for these people was in seeing others living a normal life and using them as models for their own desired behavior.

THE ASSESSMENT

After taking note of the psychological and emotional damages caused by the trauma of unemployment, I realized that I had a very important choice to make. I could see the negative effects of what had happened to me as well as the potential for things to get much worse. I felt changes in my family and friends and most strongly in myself. The choice I had to make was on the type of course I would follow in the immediate period of time to come. Would I be bitter, angry, and cynical? Or, would I accept the facts and move on? Would I condemn the world and everything in it? Or, would I look for a brighter side of life? In short, was my cup to be half empty or half full?

The simplicity of the question does not realistically reflect the complexity of arriving at a decision. To be honest and fair with myself, I had to somehow change hats and try to consider some potentially positive effects of this crisis. As evidenced by the previous pages illuminating the far-reaching negative realities, this kind of magical change did not come easily for me. I knew, however, that such a choice was mine to make and if it was to be made, I wanted it to be done with as much consideration as possible.

As a fact of life, unemployment represented two dramatic changes for me almost immediately. First, the idle time meant I could consider future actions and directions without interruption. While working full-time, there never seemed to be either the need or ability to seriously think about changing careers or jobs. Without a job to go to each day, I could read about new vocations, changing employment trends and salaries, and other things that I could never seem to find time for while working. One friend I spoke with found this idleness the worst aspect about being unemployed. For him, each working day had meant a full schedule with many appointments and commitments. This gone, he was unable to occupy his time with thoughts of anything but getting another job—any job.

The second change I felt very quickly was the disappearance of any job-related pressures to which I had grown so accustomed. While working, I was becoming increasingly aware of the tensions of each day. I was responsible for more things and I always pushed to have these done well and on time. I often worked at night and on weekends. Without the job, I was less tense and now felt able to think things through more clearly. If a person is excited by the thought of late-night phone calls, this lack of activity in the evenings will again be very difficult to put up with.

For both of these points, I needed to decide if I felt either challenged or threatened. Would the time to consider new careers and options be a challenge that I could strive to make the best of? Or, would it be such a threat that I would take the first job that came along and forget all personal needs? Would the lack of tension and job-related pressures be a challenge to me to become productive in other ways? Or, would it be such a threat that I would simply watch TV or drink beer or waste the time away in bitterness?

There were some risks involved in deciding upon a new career path. If the choice required a great deal of time retraining, I might have to change my lifestyle dramatically while pursuing it. Also, there would be no guarantee of success afterward. On the other hand, a new career, based on my past training, experiences, interests, and strengths could be ultimately more rewarding both personally and financially. If I wished to stay in the identical field I had been pushed out of, I would have to make only the primary adjustment of a new job with a new company. This would entail the least amount of effort on my part, but the likelihood would remain that the job would not be a very secure or challenging one.

In deciding on a new road to take, the reassessing of goals and values can be both helpful and personally challenging. Priorities sometimes change and these changes also represent challenges or threats, depending on how they are viewed. If monetary worth and material possessions had once been more important than family closeness, this may be interchanged after a period of unemployment. If there had never been a concern about savings or planning for the future, this may become a high priority. Similarly, if money had once been of little or no concern, it may be a strong factor in reorganizing priorities. All of these potential changes, I found, could be either enhancing or debilitating, depending once again, upon how I might choose to look at them.

A discussion on choice-making and responsibility would offer nothing new here. The impact of losing a job and being unemployed for a sustained period of time is tremendous. The negative effects on not only the individual, but his or her family and friends alike can be seen in cities as well as rural communities. Even if we cannot ultimately decide our own fate, we certainly can exercise some control on the way it affects us. After the experience I have described up to this point, and after considering the future implications of what was happening, I chose to view the events as a test, though a very severe one, of my own character strength. Each experience represented a new challenge for me. I may not have been a carpenter, but I believed I could learn to be one if I wished to or felt forced into being one. Likewise, I may not have been employed, but I believed I would be someday and I continued to do everything in my power to make that happen.

With each day that passed, I was better able to recognize hurdles in my life and slowly I gained control of them. Ultimately, I wished that there would be no one unemployed or in fear of losing his or her job. I recognized, however, that this might never become a reality. In the meantime, I tried to be as active a player in my own life as possible and not a passive spectator who just let it all go by.

chapter six

Starting Over

Up to this time in the life of an unemployed person, four major events have occurred that provide a springboard for either growth or deterioration. First, and foremost, the job has been lost. However the circumstances may have taken place, the result is the same—unemployed. Second, family and friends have been made aware of the new life situation and resulting changes have been set in motion. Third, the necessary agencies and government bureaus have been contacted or registered with so that some form of assistance can be obtained. Fourth, a period of reflection and self-assessment has gone by that should aid in seeing the actual damages done to others and to the life of an unemployed individual. For me, this period signaled the real beginning of any long-term substantial changes or adjustments. Much of what comprises the remainder of this chapter, and more particularly the stages of normalization, is the result of observations and generalizations made through interaction with many others who were, like me, unemployed for the first time. The outcomes have not always been positive and the process is not an absolute guarantee for growth. Distinctions have been made at points that were most obvious to me but I am certain there are exceptions to the descriptions I offer just as there are grey areas between each stage. I offer the information as a guide or scale to help assess the personal growth or deterioration that may occur as a result of the crisis of unemployment.

Armed with new life experiences and information, a major time of reorganization begins, ultimately leading to either personal fulfillment or emotional and psychological stagnation and ruin. Though the amount of time required to move through this process is unique for each individual, the actual existence of it is very common to people experiencing such a traumatic separation. In some respects, this process of normalization can be likened to the grieving process of death and dying. The powerlessness and futility of what is happening tends to accent feelings of anger, fear, and resentment. Just as impending death for a cancer patient forces the reorganization of his or her life, so, too, does losing a job mark the beginning of some major changes in the life of an unemployed person.

Both the unemployed and their families experience the effects of a transition from stage to stage of this process. While it is important that each period be experienced and dealt with effectively, becoming mired in one may be disruptive to the successful completion of the total process and thus may limit an individual's potential to regain his or her balance in life. It must be added, above all else, that this is a normal and psychologically healthy process. In fact, it is only the denial or ignorance of its necessity that is really dangerous to a person. By understanding and accepting the reality of the stages of normalization, each person is able to move through them more effectively and also help others during similarly difficult times.

THE FIVE-C'S OF NORMALIZATION

Concession

This initial stage is, perhaps, the most critical point for any successful reorganization in the life of an unemployed person. It necessarily involves an objective and realistic acceptance of what has happened. The job is actually gone; there is no longer a regular paycheck; there is nowhere to go each morning and nothing to do; to these facts, there is no denial or false hope given. Upon reflection, a clear understanding of why all of this has occurred can begin to emerge. For example, the severe downturn in our national economy may have been the sole determining influence on being released. However, there may have also been political, or interpersonal, causes as well. These may have been the result of management changes or corporate restructuring, personality differences, or an owner's inability to create or redesign a new job description. Finally, the release may have come largely as the result of poor performance on the job. Without rationalizing or trying to excuse substandard work, the unemployed individual can learn a great deal to help him or herself in future positions if this, in fact, was the cause of the departure.

This period can also be uncomfortable for a person who is just beginning to try and take responsibility for his or her life. To concede the obvious is not easy at times, and to accept some of the blame for being without work may likewise be difficult. If poor work quality was the cause for being fired, it may be very hard to pour any further energy into not feeling so inadequate. Many changes occur at this stage in the process, and final acceptance of reality may be long in coming. Apart from the individual, there is a need for family members or even some very close friends to gain a clear and realistic acceptance of the reality of another person being without a job. The need to understand what happened and to take whatever responsibility is required is paramount in moving on to the other stages of normalization.

In conversations with people both employed and unemployed a few glaring examples developed that illustrate my own reluctance to accept this reality as well as a similar reluctance on the parts of others recently unemployed. Because of the unwillingness to let go, or start over, it is sometimes easier to maintain some kind of attachment, even if it is irrational, to an old job or company. This tendency can be seen in those who foster thoughts of someday returning to the old job, even though this may be a very remote possibility. These individuals may also maintain a personal relationship with an old boss, former colleagues, or even their own replacement. Unaware of the uneasiness they create around them, they seek the slightest possibility of security even at the cost of personal degradation and humiliation. On occasion I found myself making comments such as "*We* sold that job," or "*We* make that line," or "*We* have the best products and prices." With thoughts such as those, little acceptance of the situation was occurring. In a related vein, if people around me continued to talk about jobs that they just lost or were going back to, my tendency was to fall into a similar pattern of thoughts. Because this was a precarious time, anything that tended to help escape its reality seemed acceptable.

Keeping in mind the deep loss of security caused by unemployment, along with the feelings of personal inadequacy and fear of impending changes in life, for the unemployed the reality of objective acceptance of what has happened, and why, can become a "straw to break the camel's back." Nevertheless, this time of honest reflection and concession is vital to the successful reorganization or rebuilding of personal meaning in life.

For some, this stage may take a long time. A dysfunctional support system of angry or fearful friends, the hostility felt in government offices and the nonsense of bureaucratic involvement, tend to stifle any quick movement through this stage. Of final consideration is the effect that the healthy component of anger may have on an individual during this period. In order to understand its source and deal most effectively with it, this type of anger must be differentiated from that provided by others. Anger can be healthy and growth-oriented when it is directed toward things that warrant it. To feel constant hostility or resentment toward people who drive nice cars or have secure jobs serves no healthy end. However, when the anger of others is allowed to influence too great a portion of a person's perceptions, such feelings may abound. By contrast, to the person who feels he or she has been purposely degraded or injured, anger is a justified reaction. This does not mean that anger lasts forever or results in mayhem, but it is certainly an honest reaction to a perceived event. As final acceptance of this life situation is completed, the transition into the second stage begins.

Condemnation

Because the crisis of unemployment seems often to be the result of events or circumstances totally beyond the control of the person most directly affected, a great deal of anger and resentment usually develop from the helpless or futile feelings that accompany it. To have, ultimately, such little control over something so vitally important to so many areas of a person's life is a very hard realization to accept. You may feel angry both at yourself for being in such a situation and at many others who, you feel, helped cause it. This period of expressed anger is a functionally healthy time of life. To be upset about actual events and real feelings is natural, and to deny any effect of such internal reality is unhealthy.

Your own checklist of what seems to be legitimate causes for hostility may become longer as you begin to let out some of the pent-up feelings of resentment. For a short time, you may find that you need little encouragement or support from others to become very angry. On the contrary, when family or friends become as upset as you, you may resent them distracting from your own expression of such feelings. After all, you have a right to be mad about being unemployed. In retrospect, you may feel the owner and the company have taken unfair advantage of your loyalty and your desire to do a good job. Similarly, you may strongly resent a former employer who could sit very comfortably and secure as you are forced to rearrange your entire life—you have to seek new employment, you have to prolong starting a family, you have to cancel long-term life goals.

You also feel angry about some things that are more directly related to your own actions. Aside from feeling as though he were not in control of his life, one person realized that he had allowed a great financial dependence on a job to occur in spite of evidence he had indicating its potential effects. Shortly after he had begun to work with a company, he was told how a smart owner should encourage an employee to take on further financial obligations such as a home or family by either giving a raise or just telling the employer it was a good idea. How stupid to not see that he was a part of such a scenario only a couple of years after he was there. The purpose, he was told, for doing this was to gain greater control and loyalty from an employee as financial obligations became more dependent on the salary provided by the company. Even with this information, he was not smart enough to prevent his own dependence from occurring! Because of this error, he was forced to file for unemployment benefits, sell possessions, refinance loans and, most critically, be in part, a source of disappointment to himself and his family. Along with the anger he felt about being so short-sighted, a generalized resentment toward his former employer had built up because he felt certain that none of these things would ever happen to the owner or his family.

When accurately and justifiably placed, negative feelings such as these can be healthy. In fact, to continually deny negative feelings can result in very unhealthy and unproductive behavior. There are times when you feel your dignity has been stripped and values compromised. To be treated as just another casualty of an economic recession is like having your personal identity taken away. For this you are angry. To be treated as a failure by a bureaucracy that only understands regulations but not living people is like losing all self-esteem. For this, too, you are angry. And, to be so totally forgotten by a few long-time friends is like being mortally stabbed in the back. For this, at last, you are angry. These feelings are in order and are properly placed. The end result should be their acceptance, resolution, and release. They may occasionally recur but never to their original strength.

An even more unhealthy side of this picture can occur if anger is totally internalized and aimed only at personal qualities. An individual may become cemented in a pattern of self-abuse or neglect, which can lead to psychological suicide. If allowed to continue, this form of behavior ensures that new employment is either impossible to find or retain because of such a diminished self-concept. One individual I spoke with was very illustrative of this phenomenon. After he lost his job of many years, he began to get very angry at himself for not being a better or smarter employee. In time, this anger began to chip away at the remaining positive feelings he had for himself and his abilities. Once again hired, his own doubt about his abilities led to such self-induced pressure to perform, that he literally guaranteed his own failure. When his fear of failing became reality, it was further evidence of his inadequacy as a person. In this case, the anger and negative feelings were misdirected and led to more severe problems. If similar feelings are focused incorrectly on people or on the system they may result in difficulty with other aspects of life. To resent another person, simply because he or she may have a job is not very rational or productive. Likewise, to resent the entire bureaucratic system and all that it entails just because it seems to place a person in a position of powerlessness is also unhealthy.

Overall, the stage of condemnation may not be a very productive one in terms of reemployment or personal assessments. Potential employers are unlikely to hire someone who displays a great deal of hostility or resentment toward life in general. As far as gaining any valid insights into personal values or priorities, combating this attitude is made difficult when thoughts of retaliation or retribution fill the days of idleness. Perhaps the greatest danger during this period lies in the possibility of misdirecting negative feelings toward family members or close friends who genuinely wish to help ease pressures of the times. Doing so may eliminate the greatest source of healthy relationships at a moment when they are most needed. The swelling of negative feelings subsides as the feelings find ways into expression. Because the form of expression can be physical as well as verbal, the unemployed person must try to maintain a sense of awareness about why some new behaviors may be occurring. Physical abuse of one's self or of others is an unhealthy way of coping with the negative feelings of this stage and must not become an accepted means of the redirection of them. As this period concludes, the need to demonstrate or release the anger and resentment is much lower and it gives way to the third stage in the process of normalization.

Control

The period of control is critical during this process. After the normal and healthy expression of negative feelings, resulting from the frustration of being unemployed and feeling so powerless to do anything about it, a time is needed to reestablish priorities, relationships, and some order to daily living. This stage occurs as a feeling of self-direction is gained over the experiences of the previous stage. If likened to an overtired infant, this is the time when the uncontrolled crying ceases and sleep finally wins out over fatigue. In much the same way, the crisis of unemployment must now move from a time of anger and self-pity to more deliberate and positive activities. Accented by the healthy use of normal defense mechanisms, this stage provides a much needed diversion from the stagnating effects of negativism already experienced.

The use of rationalization occurs, allowing the emergence of positive and healthy self-perceptions. To illustrate, regardless of my role in becoming unemployed, I knew I was a loyal employee who always worked hard and continually tried to do my best. Inside me I knew I was a good person worthy of the respect given to me by friends and co-workers. If the probability was strong that poor economic conditions were the only cause of my being released, then that was reason enough for me.

Identification with others is also a useful tool during this period. As the period of unemployment goes on, opportunities to interact and socialize with people who are still working must be fostered. For some, this is done through increased church or civic involvement. By doing this, the possibilities increase that the irrational feelings of alienation, which come from being unemployed, can be countered by the acceptance of friends, or even strangers, in social settings. The identification with others is very helpful in maintaining a positive self-image and lessening the effects of feeling like a complete failure. It is important to note here that if in trying to identify with a larger group a person chooses unhealthy examples such as drug users or heavy drinkers, this choice must be viewed as a move away from growth for the individual. Escape from reality through drugs or alcohol does little to solve the long-term crisis of unemployment.

During this stage, feelings are sometimes consciously suppressed so that other things can be dealt with more effectively. There is no real denial of those feelings but little energy is given to their need for expression. After losing her job, one individual became very anxious and fearful about the future. This fear, however, she accepted and then chose to try to be as positive and optimistic as possible about the coming days. She felt that this would allow her the greatest potential in trying to start over by using her strengths instead of her weaknesses. Likewise, she chose to explore ways to keep the feelings of resentment from spilling over into other areas of her life that could offer more personal rewards and fulfillment. Both instances allowed her to focus on more productive possibilities instead of the negative components of the feelings involved. In neither case did she deny that she was either afraid or resentful, but she did choose to go on to another place in her life that offered more positive effects.

On some occasions, we may project some of our own qualities to others and fail to see the error in our thinking. However, at other times the end results may be very good. One evening while talking with a friend, I started to notice how negative and cynical his comments were becoming about each topic we discussed. It seemed that no matter how I tried to lighten the conversation he found something bad to say. In time, I grew very weary of this and finally found a way to gracefully leave. Upon reflection, I realized that I actually disliked most strongly in him, those qualities that were becoming more and more a pattern of my own behavior. I had apparently fostered in him the perception that being negative or pessimistic was an acceptable way to behave because that was how I seemed to view things. From that point on, I tried to remain conscious of things I said and how I said them. For me the result was an effort to be more genuinely aware of good things in my life and to express those as such.

A similar example was related to me by a friend who had only been unemployed for a brief period of time. It seemed that each time she met with a particular girlfriend, the topic of discussion invariably became the unsatisfying marriage her friend was having. The great amount of wallowing in self-pity became so distasteful to my friend that she ultimately chose not to see that person again. After thinking about what had happened, she too realized that the greatest difficulty for her was not as much with the complaining of her friend as with accepting her own growing feelings of self-pity. Upon recognition of this, however, she was able to try and begin to accent the positive things in her life and discount the importance of areas that seemed to be least rewarding for her. The results for her were more self-expressed recognition of the good things in her life and less genuine self-pity. In both cases, potential losses were turned into gains as feelings were dealt with honestly and accurately.

During the period of control, there is often a characteristic time of reenergizing or refueling the emotional batteries. One way in which this happens is through the healthy use of escape. Temporary diversions provide time to reorganize thoughts or reflect on past events and to begin to consider new or alternate courses. When used as a healthy means of release, activities such as reading, camping, going to a movie, or physical exercise may all represent realistic ways of providing a break from the pressures of the time. As new ideas are generated and formed, the fourth stage of the process begins.

Catharsis

This stage is characterized by the very open and honest sharing of ideas and feelings about what has happened. Information is processed for its value in personal reorganization only. There is little to be gained by maintaining or fostering feelings of resentment and anger. However, the recognition, discussion, and acceptance of these feelings by the unemployed and their families is very helpful in completing the process of normalization. Therefore, such activities should not be viewed as unhealthy or unproductive during this period. The open exchange of feelings and beliefs can be very beneficial if it occurs with others who are important in the life of the unemployed. One person found that because of the very personal nature of much of what he needed to share, he was reluctant to just open up with anyone he met. Usually, he spoke only with his wife or a couple of close friends. Without a great deal of moaning or complaining, he expressed his fears and anxieties about the future. He was not certain his marriage could withstand the pressure of changes he thought would have to be made. He was insecure about maintaining his friendships because he could no longer afford to do the things with his friends that he had been doing. He was unsure of his ability to find another job and earn enough to fulfill his long-term dream of a family. He also knew that starting over would not be easy. He needed and wanted the encouragement of others. Although he feared failing again, or feeling like a failure, he knew he had to risk that possibility and try to again be employed.

Ultimately, his fears and uncertainties went unfulfilled. There was more strength in his marriage than he thought, and his friends had more faith in him and his abilities than he had given them credit for. The opportunity to share his anxieties with others, however, offered the single most personally rewarding experience during this period of his life. It served to dispel some anxieties and strengthen some ties which, without it, would probably have been viewed much differently in the overall picture. This stage, when preceded by the first three, offers an optimum opportunity to learn from previous experiences and brainstorm about future possibilities. Because it is a time characterized by nonthreatening exchange, input from others can help this become a very productive period in the process of normalization.

Challenge

In comparison to the previous stages, this is the most productive and action-oriented period of time leading up to reemployment. The clarification of values and ordering of priorities constitute a tremendous challenge to both the old ways of thinking and the new directions to be considered. Previously held beliefs about employment, security, and loyalty may be challenged in light of the present crisis being experienced. This is a time to explore alternatives and new ideas. If either law school or carpentry were once far-removed fantasies, this may be the best time to seriously consider each.

Through the reorganization of values, beliefs, goals, and priorities, new behaviors develop as such things take on new meanings. Personal freedom may be paramount where it had been unimportant before. Money or wages may represent a means to an end rather than an end in and of itself. Many choices are made during this period as an individual strives to meet the challenge of the times. However, changes do not occur instantaneously. Some things must be relearned, learned anew, or forgotten. Responses to previously held biases or concepts may be greatly altered as new behaviors become more appropriate in light of insights gained through this total experience. Before the process of normalization is complete, there are a few danger areas encountered that can cause setbacks if not handled appropriately. I have labeled these potential enemies as *snags, triggers*, and *time bombs*.

Snags. A *snag* is characterized as more of a nuisance than a major pitfall. It may tend to relate to a potentially emotional area, but unless vigorously pursued, is not very powerful in its effect on us. Most often a snag takes the form of a mundane comment or question such as "How's the job hunting going?" Because of the time needed to honestly answer such a question, the snag becomes an unnecessary diversion from more suitable topics of discussion such as family concerns or job interests or countless other things. Although the snag is not very emotionally loaded, if encountered often enough it can easily become a *trigger* for more intense reactions. Generally, these kinds of comments require little more than a passing response or recognition and can then be forgotten. During a period of condemnation or anger, snags become catalysts for long tirades that help neither the raver nor the person who is listening. In fact, on one occasion when given a clipping from the want ads of a local newspaper, I observed a friend launch into a tirade reflecting his ability to read a paper by himself very ably and therefore he did not need any patronizing favors of that person! Obviously, an apology was in order—and he made one the next day.

Triggers. *Triggers* are statements, or actions, which will draw an emotionally loaded response almost immediately. The strength of such a response is directly related to the ignorance of the comment made and how deeply it may touch a tender area. I recently attended a gathering of old friends and acquaintances, some of whom I had not seen for quite a while. During the evening I listened in on a conversation with three people about unemployment and some of the political and social aspects of it. Two of them did not know, however, that the third was unemployed. As they continued to share their thoughts and ideas, it was disclosed that one of these individuals recently started back to work after a prolonged period of unemployment. The other person had never been in such a situation and was, in fact, in what he felt to be a very secure position. While the one person cursed the time he spent without work, the other slowly began to raise questions about the necessity of anyone being unemployed if he or she really wanted a job. For the person who was secure and inexperienced in the world of unemployment, the solution to such a problem was very simple. Anyone without a job could become either a real estate or insurance salesperson! By working on straight commission, employers would quickly hire such a person and then it would become merely a question of how hard an individual chose to work as to how successful he or she might be. To him, hard work equaled reward equaled a secure job. Needless to say, such a conversation triggered many things within the third individual, but being aware of his own short fuse in that area greatly aided him in presenting two rational questions for consideration. First, he asked if enough concrete evidence (such as the fact there are approximately 20 million under- or unemployed) could be amassed to refute the notion that the problem of unemployment could be settled by everyone becoming a salesperson who works strictly on commission, would he change his belief? The second person's response, after a brief period of consideration, was no, he would not change his mind in spite of information to the contrary. The second question to him then was how did he get the evidence to support his belief in the first place. To this, he could only answer it was just what he chose to believe. Confronted with such narrowness and shallowness, the third person realized that any further involvement with the second person at that moment would be futile and would likely lead into the final danger area of time bombs.

Time Bombs. These are the most sensitive areas of our feelings and thoughts which, if shaken too vigorously, will blow up. They are the ideas and beliefs we tend to deal with in very private and personal ways such as our perceptions of marriage and fidelity, parenting and punishment, or being a sole-supporting breadwinner. Many chauvinistic beliefs become time bombs because they leave little room for the acceptance of emotional or weaker aspects of the male personality. The power of the reaction released by a time bomb is related to the sensitivity of the area affected. For example, I listened to a conversation at the unemployment office one day between two young men in their midtwenties. One asked the other how he and his family were making out without him working. The response to this was that his wife was working part-time to help buy food and pay rent but it was getting harder to make ends meet. With disbelief in his voice, the first person instructed the second that he should stop acting so proud and go on welfare to get money and food stamps. At this, the second individual exploded. His feeling was that it was bad enough that he could not provide for his family by himself, but to go on welfare would strip the last thread of dignity from him.

This individual was not an example of someone who had refused to face the facts and accept them or who had depressed any anger he felt about being unemployed. For him, an unexploded time bomb laid in his perceptions and values about his role as a husband and father in a family relationship. Unfortunately, I have observed similar episodes in government offices where individuals may be asking for assistance for the first time in their lives and some counselors or other personnel walk across such sensitive areas. Diffusing the time bombs within us is not easy. Generally, these are the result of years and years of religious or social belief systems. Although most of us have some areas like these within us, they are usually controlled by recognizing their power and carefully dealing with them. One of the saddest statistics related to the reality of rising unemployment is the increasing evidence of suicide and physical abuse of children or family members. The time bombs would appear to be going off more frequently. The need for us to recognize and treat these areas accordingly is growing with the ever-increasing number of people who are not only unemployed, but others who may be living in real fear of becoming unemployed.

The period of challenge is completed as an awareness grows enabling us to understand and deal with the many feelings and pitfalls experienced during this entire experience. The real challenge, I feel, is a personal one: Will you, with all of the knowledge and insight you have gained about what is happening and might happen in the future, let yourself be destroyed by this crisis? Or, using the information you now have, will you strive to be as positive about life as you can and become as productive as possible? For some, this challenge either fails to materialize or it ceases to exist and becomes apparent in the hopeless expressions on their faces and their slumped shoulders. Yet others accept the challenge and seek ways to maintain a sense of pride and dignity in spite of an economic recession or government processes that tend to foster more dependency than strength.

CONSIDERING REEMPLOYMENT

Starting over could never be possible without a period of time spent considering the realities of reentering the work force. Not only are there many concrete and obvious points to think about, but new and subtle facts now exist that can have a very strong effect on choices and outcomes. Getting into the mainstream of things and learning new techniques, questions to ask, and tendencies to beware of are areas that must be explored and evaluated.

Beginning the Search

To the newly unemployed, there would appear to be a number of good vehicles for getting back into the flow of things.

As might be expected, the most obvious of these is the newspaper want-ad section. In major cities this is often extensive, regardless of its content. Another possibility lies in the use of government offices or departments designed specifically for helping the unemployed find jobs. In some areas of the country, the listings in these offices are available to be seen without the need for actually seeing a counselor. Apart from but similar to the public agencies available are a vast number of private placement centers which, for a fee, will attempt to place unemployed individuals in any one of their well-protected jobs. Becoming more visible are companies that promise the moon, but in essence deliver little more than a mailing service for nicely typed and smartly worded résumés. A last source of useful leads or ideas about jobs may be found in the existing circle of friends already associated with an unemployed person. One more personal reference may prove invaluable in times such as these.

All in all, however, these sources tend to become exhausted quite quickly. I found the want ads to be a fair supplier of initial leads, but not one substantial possibility resulted from the numerous inquiries I made in areas of sales, part-time, and even general labor positions. Somebody may have been getting these jobs, but it wasn't me. In terms of public placement assistance, when I worked in a government office a number of years ago, I found that most of the actual success stories were the result of client-found employment, and therefore I question the real ability of these agencies to provide little more than short-term or transient positions. From time to time, good jobs do appear, however, so you should not completely rule out this option. Private agencies require fees that are, on occasion, paid by the new employers but most often, are the responsibility of a new employee. For some jobs the fees themselves are prohibitive, so you may not wish to use this source yourself. Last, even an extended circle of friends cannot be expected to keep their energies high in a search for a job opening for someone they may not see frequently. Perhaps the necessary virtues of beginning such a search lie in patience, persistence, optimism, and self-direction. All of these may be severely tested, however, as time passes and no positive results occur.

Techniques

There are numerous private agencies that will, for a substantial sum, prepare a professional résumé to be used in seeking a job. If you had been with one company for a long period, you may have no appreciation for what preparing a résumé entails or what the preferred styles are for the type of job you are seeking. My own research led me to believe that a résumé done well could be a big plus toward getting a job, while a poorly prepared one could be a great distraction. Done either personally or professionally, a résumé should be both creative and informative without being too wordy or esoteric. Quite a challenge for an ill-prepared applicant!

Aside from the ignorance of preparing a quality résumé that shows past experience, membership in organizations, and educational background, you may also be at a loss about how to update old placement files or how to go about obtaining new letters of reference. An initial concern with even using references is whether or not to suggest your last employer as a source. Even if you have no evidence to indicate a bad evaluation might be forthcoming, your anxieties may lead you to fear this possibility. On the other hand, it certainly would seem odd to not use any reference from such a large time period as may have gone by. Others I have spoken with absolutely refused to list their last employer as a reference because of the certainty of a poor report. In the last analysis, it is probably best to list all previous experience and give a personal reference for each. If nothing else, this will present a continuous work history that might be more beneficial in the long run than conspicuously omitting a segment.

KNEE-JERK TENDENCIES

From the sometimes sudden and unexpected act of losing a job, I discovered three almost universal, immediate reflex tendencies in many newly unemployed individuals. These beliefs, though largely irrational, can become a source of prolonged discomfort if not dealt with effectively. The first is a strong conviction that the best course to follow is to seek reemployment in the very same field as was just left. When this is done to the exclusion of all other possibilities, there develops a great danger that no similar work exists and any diversion to some other field will necessarily seem to be forced and unwanted. To seriously consider the possibility of a new line of work or profession does require a certain amount of courage. At a time when personal and financial pressures seem so great, this courage may be hard to muster, but the likelihood of "being painted into a corner" is likewise great and should be guarded against as much as possible. There is a vast difference between a computer programmer choosing to seek work in that field only and an anthropology teacher who feels that the only suitable job to seek is as a teacher of anthropology. To the programmer with such a belief the odds are fair that he or she will not be disappointed; the teacher, however, will likely encounter a great deal of trouble finding identical work.

The second major reflex tendency is to let a private employment agency find you suitable work. In the first weeks of being unemployed, I spoke with various individuals at private agencies. I found not only were the fees high and the results without guarantee, but the competition was very keen for fewer, less desirable jobs. However, because of the amount of energy required to maintain order in a person's life during this period, relying on a private agency may be the only realistic means of obtaining suitable work. It should be pointed out, however, that a private agency receives a commission for the placement of an individual in a job and often there is little incentive for providing the best match-up of these two components. Therefore, it is quite possible that either a job or an applicant can be overstated, thus resulting in a poor placement and potential failure.

The final reflex tendency I noticed upon losing a job was to lessen the impact by believing that there are always openings for salespeople of one sort or another. More than one person I encountered at the unemployment office let me know that as soon as the benefits expired they would start selling cars, books, clothes, or something else. True or not, such a casual approach to this situation cannot do much to keep it from recurring. If you study the want ads and job notices, you may see many jobs listed for various salespeople. If you have had a long and successful history in selling, you may feel that any of those could be yours for a song. The reality, however, is that for sales jobs the competition is as keen as it is for most other lines of work. More and more highly qualified, excellent people are applying for fewer and fewer, lower-paying, less rewarding jobs.

TO TAKE IT OR NOT TO TAKE IT

After rediscovering the best ways to apply for a job and the best places to obtain leads, and after overcoming the initial reactions of being suddenly unemployed, the possibility presents itself that a job may be offered and a decision must be made about it. At this point, there are a number of serious questions to be considered that will hopefully enhance the probability that a productive relationship will grow for both the employee and the employer.

Some immediate things to look for center around the need for long-term job security. Is this a growth company? Is it very vulnerable to fads or changes in the economy? What kind of retirement, profit-sharing, or long-term benefits are available? After many weeks of seeking employment, these kinds of questions lose most of their thunder. The need for security gives way to the need to be productive and earn a wage. In this context, it is necessary to consider some other very basic points as well. Do you need to retrain? If so, will you be paid during this time or will the employer pay for the outside training? Also, how long will retraining take and what benefits are available during this period? You need to also assess your own capabilities, although by this time just about anything may seem possible.

In terms of the job itself, you will want to know the kinds of social interactions expected of you. You may be reluctant to again enter into a close personal relationship with the owner, but if necessity dictates this, you must be ready to try. The final question to pose is are you taking a job purely for the money with little thought given to compromising personal beliefs or values?

These kinds of points are extremely difficult to give serious consideration to when there is little or no income and living expenses are not being met. During such times, any job will be acceptable. The most you can hope for under the circumstances is a chance to regain some self-respect and earn enough money to establish a normal standard of living once again. The question of "to take it or not to take it" may not exist for all people who become unemployed. However, if it exists for some, it is a short-lived luxury at best.

Up to this point, the primary focus of this book has been upon the events, the changes, the feelings, and the processes that go on in the life of an unemployed individual. Attention has been drawn to the effects of unemployment on a person's family and close friends but little has been said about the role of the larger society during this life crisis. In order to complete the process now underway and answer the question, "Is there life after unemployment?", a few more general areas must be brought into the picture. It is necessary to consider the perceptions about work and working, which at times seem to govern so much of the behavior we either observe in others or engage in ourselves. If, in fact, there is a life after becoming unemployed, perhaps it is characterized by views of the world of work that are totally alien to those previously held.

chapter seven

Unemployed or Unemployable?

A major contributing factor to effectively dealing with the life crisis of unemployment is a clear understanding of what is happening both in the world around us and within our own minds. This clarity, however, is often impossible to attain on one's own especially if beliefs, values, and attitudes have been generally founded upon information not totally accurate. Sharing ideas with friends and others serves to enrich the pool of knowledge a person is able to draw upon when trying to determine new ways of dealing with the surrounding world. In such exchanges, it becomes possible to either test new thoughts, reaffirm old beliefs, or form different perceptions of previously held concepts. Without this kind of interaction, there is a strong tendency to maintain previously held beliefs, which may be ineffective in dealing with this new life situation.

    Much of the difficulty I have seen others experience in trying to cope with being unemployed is in part a result of the belief in a number of myths, or misconceptions, which strongly affect how this crisis is being perceived. An interesting characteristic of a myth is that it seems to have some faint hint of truth or plausibility that makes it so believable. It seems to gain credibility through the least amount of actual truth and once it becomes established as a basis for other beliefs, is almost self-perpetuating. With the ever-changing circumstances of today's world, new myths are sometimes quickly formed and before long begin to strongly influence a person's behavior or even an entire belief system. Because people treat a myth as truth, they tend to behave as if it were. This serves to reinforce the plausibility of it and thus aids in its continued belief.

While some myths are not necessarily evil or debilitating, anything that serves to alter or prevent the accurate perception of a life situation such as being unemployed is not good. I would never argue the perpetuation of the belief in a tooth-fairy. Now, however, I find great difficulty in accepting a notion such as the myth of tenure for educators. Youngsters lessen their fear of impending pain or embarrassment about losing a tooth with a belief of gaining some special gift or favor from an imaginary person. Adults, on the other hand, who base an entire belief system on a previously unquestioned truth such as tenure are apt to find their lives socially, financially, professionally, and personally devastated by the reality of an entire college faculty being reorganized. For these people, life will never be the same. This fact alone suggests the basis of a second major myth being fostered in the minds of many people today. That is that a job, in and of itself, will solve all of the problems of an unemployed person. More detailed discussion of this myth will follow, but I use these two examples to illustrate how one partial-truth may lead to another one and in so doing create an even greater danger of forming still others.

You may be asking yourself, "Why this discussion about myths? What does this have to do with me?" To this point, those appear to be timely questions. The answer, in part, lies in the need to gain a clear understanding of the kinds of beliefs that may influence the behavior of other people. But, more important, gaining insight into the causes of some of our own acts is invaluable in learning to cope with present difficulties and preventing future ones. For example, if I can predict your actions based upon your demonstrated beliefs about unemployment, I will be able to either gain from you some insight I do not already have or prevent you from influencing my beliefs by moving away from you. By becoming aware of some common myths that revolve around the world of work, around finding a job, or around unemployment you can determine to what extent they may already affect your own behavior or the behavior of others. In the last analysis, how such myths are perceived may be the primary difference between actually being "unemployed" or feeling "unemployable."

What follows are some common myths I have identified and some others suggested to me. These originate in the three primary areas of work, working, and trying to find work. It is important to understand that personal awareness of such misconceptions rarely causes changes in "other" individuals who may hold these beliefs as truth. It may, however, be quite helpful in learning to either cope with or work around such people and, thus, make the life of the unemployed a little more bearable.

MYTHS ABOUT WORKING

In initially listing three major myths of this category, some cause may be discovered as to why a job was lost in the first place. If the loss seemed to be a result of some very ambiguous reasons, these myths, if viewed through the eyes of the employer, may provide a more insightful view of what actually occurred. Many bosses, foremen, owners, and so on consider the role of competition as it relates to the effectiveness of a business as the sole determinant of success or failure. An employee who thrives on doing the best job he or she can possibly do and needs no comparisons made to co-workers is an enigma to such an employer. The myth on the part of the owner is that competition will motivate all workers to do more work and thus increase productivity. Because productivity ultimately represents profits to a business, it is something to continually strive for, or so believe some people. Although research does not support this belief in the long run, the boss encourages one employee to do more than another. If a particular worker seems to be uninterested in such competition and still does an above-average job, the boss is faced with a dilemma. He may allow this rebel to continue while imploring other workers to compete, or he may eliminate the thorn from his side and thus perpetuate the myth more uniformly. If the worker in question is aware of the employer's belief in this area, he or she can do things to maintain his or her job. These actions may range from paying token lip-service to showing enthusiastic support of the competition between workers.

The second myth about working is that competition guarantees a higher quality of work or final product. The missing dimension here, however, is that it also ensures that a percentage of all work will be labeled "unfit," "fail," or "reject." When an employer believes he or she must have only the most efficient, quality-minded workers, he or she will try to eliminate those who cannot produce the best final product. If a worker is aware of this need for quality, he or she may be able to bargain for adequate time to guarantee such a first-rate performance. For owners who believe so strongly in quality, quantity is sometimes negotiable. To retain a job, an employee may need to pursue any opening and this may be one.

The final myth about working is that everyone, by nature, is competitive so having similar behavior in the world of work is the best way to get things done. Again, as a myth easily disproven simply by the observation of the cooperation that takes place in any work place, it is nonetheless a strong influence on some employers or bosses. As an employee, if this is understood as having a distinct effect on how an owner makes decisions, it can be utilized for the optimum results. One worker might offer suggestions on how to compete with other companies more effectively or efficiently, while another worker might refrain from this kind of activity altogether and perhaps diminish his or her likelihood of being retained if a choice were to be made between the two. Again, the purpose of recognizing the ways an employer, or boss, may be personally influenced is not necessarily to change those beliefs but to be able to contend with them in ways that can best retain a job without being too devious or totally dishonest.

In retrospect, these myths may offer little satisfaction in discovering why a job was lost. The major consideration of economic hard times often seems to explain quite clearly the cause for being laid off. However, when such a cause is not so apparent, the subtle suggestions offered may serve to further explain why one person is unemployed. Hopefully, such awareness may help to see that a similar event will not recur on future jobs.

MYTHS ABOUT WORK

Adding to the difficulty of adjusting to a prolonged period of unemployment are two general myths that seem to be held by many unemployed people. The first and most painful fact to experience is that it is not always the "other" person who is laid off, furloughed, or otherwise loses his or her job. There is a strong wish to believe that only unnamed or unknown people lose jobs and within this desire lives the myth. To really think that you might be the next name drawn to be fired is very disquieting. Because of the tendency to ignore the possibility of being unemployed, the reality of it becomes even more unsettling. Even though one particular person was not naive to the events going on around him or to the economic pressures of the building and construction industry, he held fast to the belief that it could not happen to him. Such a belief only magnified the trauma he experienced upon being told he was being let go.

The second general myth, which adds greatly to the pain of losing a job, is a belief that there does exist, somewhere or somehow, any real job security. This myth is typified by the notion of tenure for educators. In the past months I have spoken with many professors who are without jobs because of a reorganization of an entire college faculty. For them, a dream was totally shattered and their world turned upside down. Reality has demonstrated to them that no real job security exists for tenured staff regardless of credentials or years of experience. If the revenues cannot support the overhead, even time-honored positions can be eliminated.

One final myth I observed in the thinking of many people centers around a belief that if only a job were made available for each person who wanted and needed one the problem of unemployment would cease. This idea is received as truth by numerous individuals some of whom are unemployed, but most of whom are working. The dangers in such a myth are great. It tends to oversimplify the extent of the far-reaching negative effects of unemployment. A job alone will not restore a sense of loyalty in a worker who feels he or she has been arbitrarily laid off. It will not promote his or her creative talents in a new job if there is no sense of security. Last, a job alone will not ensure the full use of personal strengths and skills that help to create a sense of pride about a job well done. Without the changes in perceptions necessary to accept and move beyond such myths, the life of the unemployed remains uncertain and fragmented. For those who have not experienced first-hand a prolonged period of unemployment, this myth serves two unfortunate ends. First, there is little appreciation for what may actually be happening to an unemployed neighbor. Second, there can be a tendency to discount the importance of keeping a relatively secure job during a very insecure period. In this case, an unrealistic view of the job market is created and a decision to change jobs may be made at an extremely poor time.

MYTHS ABOUT FINDING WORK

Some people contend that finding work should not be too difficult with so many jobs listed in the want ads of every metropolitan Sunday paper. This contention is based on a myth that lies in the fact that want ads reflect only the expressed needs, or interests, of employers while they say nothing about the employment potential of individuals. Ten thousand jobs in the field of high-technology listed in Flint, Michigan or Wheeling, West Virginia demonstrate nothing about the probability of a laid-off auto or mine worker to find a job in such a vocation. Also, if the claims of private employment agencies are to be accepted, most available jobs never even appear in want ads. In either case, believing such a myth about the ease of finding another job because of the number of listings in a newspaper is not productive.

Another rapidly emerging myth, which seems to be finding a warm reception, is that proper training will make the difference in getting hired for a particular job. In the past, just the opposite has been known to happen. Individuals with too much training would be passed over for fear of their resistance to retraining or learning new procedures. While training remains vitally important, experience and personal recommendations may be more critical to getting a job in today's market. The old cliché, "It's not *what* you know, it's *who* you know," is very relevant in today's job market. On one occasion a feat of heroic courage brought about a phone call from the President of the United States. The timely and well-placed call was able to serve as the recommendation necessary to provide a greatly needed job for a well-deserving individual. I fear that without the call both the job and the person would have gone separate ways, regardless of the courageous demonstration.

I have listed and illustrated a number of myths that seem to have a great impact on the life of an unemployed person. Although these may affect each individual in unique ways, the end results are often the same. They contribute greatly to the illusion of job security and thereby increase the pain experienced when it is lost. They tend to create a false sense of optimism that the government, or the system, is taking care of the problem of unemployment and therefore there is little to be concerned with. Such false perceptions may prevent the realistic assessment of a person's own skills and abilities. Because of this perception, retraining may be ignored or potential careers eliminated before they are even considered. Continuing to believe or act the way a person has always believed or acted in the past simply because it is thought to be best is another example of maintaining the belief in a myth that can prove to be very unproductive. Though past performance may validly justify repeating a process, new experiences and situations often demand new ideas and actions.

After thinking about what may have already happened, you may feel forced to accept the fact that it could happen again. Because of this, you should consider, more seriously, future goals and needs. In this regard, you should not confine possibilities for employment to only the kinds of things you have done in the past. You may be forced once again to look at skills, abilities, and interests in new and different ways. You may have to consider seriously the possibility of doing two or more things at once. Although you may sense in some government employees a genuine desire to help you become reemployed, you should not ignore the cumbersome and wasteful practices of the agencies or bureaus involved, which may tend to diminish faith in any substantial help occurring. These points may represent a significant change in perceptions that have come about as the result of an awareness of and sensitivity to the kinds of myths that influence your thinking and the thinking of others around you. In trying to dispel the misconceptions presented, there are a number of useful approaches that seem to be effective in allowing a person to gain a more accurate picture of him or herself and his or her situation.

DISPELLING A MYTH

The most obvious and sure-fire way to correct the false thinking of a myth is with facts, facts, and more facts. The truth is the best tool to use in helping to arrive at decisions or trying out new ideas. In the example of the myth of tenure for teachers, a small amount of research into the laws governing the operation of colleges or universities or even the employment contract itself would provide ample information to demonstrate that any faculty member, given the proper circumstances, could be released from any position. This truth may be very difficult to accept, but by doing so, the possibility of becoming unemployed is made a little more real and steps can be taken to contend with such an occurrence.

Myths are also dispelled by hard work and personal involvement. This is sometimes called going through the "school of hard knocks," but the result is the same. Getting involved with unemployment offices, welfare agencies, or other government services can be very uncomfortable, but in a short time it becomes apparent that there is not a great deal of potential in these places and so energies must be channeled into other areas. Also, answering ads, or going to interviews, or being completely retrained becomes accepted as less than the best solution as each is tried a few times.

Much can be gained by listening to others who have been through similar experiences and already know what is fact and what is fantasy. When told by someone more knowledgeable than I that I needed to be sure to bring certain forms along or nothing would be accomplished at a job center, I was quick to do it. As it turned out, he was correct, I had the forms, and all went as it was intended. Similar insights can be gained from people who have tried to use private agencies in getting a new job or others who have lost jobs in seemingly recession-proof occupations.

The last, but certainly not least, method of benefit in dispelling myths is the use of good, common sense. For example, if a Washington, D.C. Sunday paper has over thirty pages of want ads, and a California paper over fifty, common sense should tell you two things. One, those ads probably have nothing to do with changing your plight. And, two, homebuilders, auto workers, and steel manufacturers from all over the country are not going to flock to Washington, D.C. or California and be able to get jobs in a high-technology field.

I suspect that other myths exist that may cloud a person's thinking from time to time. However, by trying to gain a clear perception of what is real and what is imagined, you may be better able to cope with being unemployed. Much is gained and little, if anything, is lost from this process and I recommend it to others who may be similarly out of work. For me, I felt that by striving to understand as clearly as possible all that was happening in my life I was more likely to be temporarily *unemployed* as opposed to being more permanently *unemployable*.

BEING "UNEMPLOYED"

The term *unemployed*, I am convinced, was invented as a means to label and thereby categorize a certain individual who is eligible for various government services or assistance. This separates from the general population an otherwise normal, productive, fully functioning human being. Although being unemployed is only a legal status in the eyes of the bureaucracy, in effect it means much more than that to the people involved.

Just to be in a state of forced idleness strikes at some of the deepest values of an *unemployed* individual. A person who has always had an appreciation for the Protestant work ethic becomes very uncomfortable when there is no equal exchange of a fair wage for a job well done. Receiving assistance from government programs without actually working rubs against the moral grain of someone who has worked for everything he or she has ever gotten.

An *unemployed* person is in a constant search for work of any kind that allows him or her to earn the money necessary to meet financial obligations. The sense of commitment and trust is very high as the *unemployed* individual recognizes that he or she may be depended upon by others for his or her own livelihood and well-being. This kind of value system does not allow for extreme selectivity in considering the kind of work that is acceptable. A job merely provides a means to meet obligations and gain some sense of personal security and self-satisfaction through things that can be done with earned wages.

An *unemployed* person is not encumbered with myths about jobs, about working, about finding work, or about their own personal needs. Because of this, he or she is able to make choices based on a fundamental acceptance of the way life is and how he or she may want it to become. Overall, the unemployed have a mentally healthy and potentially productive view of their situation. The mental and physical discomfort of being without a job is seen more as a life challenge than a personal threat to ego or self-satisfaction. By contrast, the unemployed represent a much greater segment of the population than those labeled *unemployable*.

BEING "UNEMPLOYABLE"

Just as the term *unemployed* is used to label, categorize, and otherwise separate a particular person from the rest of the population, I am likewise convinced that the term *unemployable* was created for the same purpose. However, this is where the similarity ends between these two words. In fact, generally speaking, the unemployable possess characteristics exactly opposite of those of the unemployed. Although it may appear that some people who are labeled *unemployable* are that way as the result of circumstances outside of their own control, the truth is that fundamentally they no longer feel any value or reward in working.

To what degree the system has fostered the growth of this group through an unresponsive educational setting, inadequate training programs, or overly generous welfare grants is difficult to determine. The value of the system as it exists for the unemployable person lies in the benefits that can be gained or money that can be received. The goal for individuals who are unemployable is the same as that of the three-time losers discussed in Chapter Three. Each want to do only what is required to maintain services from as many agencies as possible.

Because of the constant state of anxiety and conflict that exists for the unemployable person, two forms of behavior can usually be observed. The first is the result of a need to run away from the source of pain or retreat from reality. In this case, a person becomes reclusive or withdrawn from others and ultimately may lose all purpose in life. Perhaps this response may help explain the rise in suicides that seems to accompany each rise in unemployment. The second type of behavior, which can usually be seen in this group, is the result of a need to strike out at a perceived threat to their existence. In this case, the belief is that "the best defense is a good offense." This person becomes abusive or angry with everyone from politicians to family members. Under these circumstances, the increased incidence of battering and child abuse is almost predictable. In either form, the results are a social and economic problem for everyone.

Unemployable individuals are a captive of inaccurate and unhealthy perceptions. Myths constitute the basis for much of their thinking. They live with a notion that all of their problems will cease and never recur, the moment that the "right" job comes along. The future is never more than one day away for this person. Because of the many misconceptions that rule the thinking of someone who is unemployable, there seems to be no order or meaning to the things that go on in his or her world. Without such meaning, little purpose exists to maintain employment, plan for a future or do things differently than in the past. In one sense, these types of people are as much victims of their own thinking as its cause. They are doomed to perpetuate the myths that exist in their lives because they represent the only kind of reasoning that is understandable or productive.

There are some large differences between being *unemployed* or being *unemployable*. A transition from the former to the latter however, can be very subtle and can occur without a person really knowing it. As weeks and months pass without work, you may start to sense changes in your own thinking that should signal danger for you. The changes begin very slowly and without some conscious effort, you may be unable to stop them before a great deal of damage has occurred. I have been able to observe such changes taking place in other unemployed people as days and weeks have passed with little or no hope for returning to work. For them, becoming unemployable was subtle and only a concentrated effort prevented it from complete reality.

DANGER SIGNALS

There were three basic clues I discovered that signal a changing view of life during this period. As time passes, you will begin to procrastinate about things that could be vitally important in becoming reemployed. If application deadlines were given in ads, you may wait until the last day to put one in. Rationally, you may feel this should not affect any chances of getting a particular job, but the fact remains that you are becoming less aggressive about seeking employment. You may also find it much more enjoyable to do things other than job-seeking activities. Your attention may be easily diverted to television, friends, or even sleeping.

The second clue is a growing negativism about yourself and of life in general. You may begin to feel defeated and unworthy for a position even before it is ever applied for. Although you never say it to a potential employer, in your mind you may think, "You don't have any openings, do you?" Accenting this increasing negativism is the fact that you begin to spend more and more time with other people who complain or gripe about their life or the world in general. This attitude is only feeding fuel to your own burning fire of pessimism and does nothing to help change your life.

The last change is a loss of self-direction. While a few short months before you may have taken a very active approach to living and interacting in the world, you now begin to become a more controlled and passive person. You might ask other people what they would do if they were in your situation. You may wait to hear from employers or placement centers instead of pursuing each for answers. You may become willing, and to some degree desire, to let other people assume responsibility for changing your life. Because of these changes, you start to view your own abilities as more narrow and limited than they actually are. These examples should serve to shake you to your senses before they become normal patterns of behavior. However, you should continue to monitor your own thoughts and actions for signs such as these so that you can prevent negative results from occurring.

As stated, the transition from unemployed to unemployable can be very subtle and difficult to remain conscious of. Hopefully, by understanding the kinds of danger signals to look for, any negative changes can be prevented completely. A fundamental distinction, which always remains between these two groups lies in the fact that the *unemployed* perceive what has happened as a *challenge* to their character strength, values, beliefs, and attitudes. The *unemployable,* on the other hand, are *threatened by* what is happening and gain little from the experience other than feeling more threatened and more inadequate.

Of the vast numbers of people out of work, most are able to maintain a relatively healthy outlook on life. If the opposite were true, and most people based their beliefs and perceptions on myths held by those around them, chaos would be ruling the country right now. By dispelling half-truths and obtaining accurate information about jobs and working, finding employment, and personal traits, an unemployed person moves into a position to change his or her life in positive ways. These changes may not necessarily result in getting another job immediately, but they will certainly provide the basis for being able to contend with the crisis of unemployment in a constructive, rather than destructive, way. Just as important, dispelling myths and reorganizing beliefs goes a long way in preparing a person for future employment. In this regard loyalty, trust, self-respect, and honesty can be qualities to be proud of rather than protective of.

In all areas of life, a person should be able to objectively ask the questions, "Where am I now?", "Where am I going?", and "How am I going to get there?" These questions should be viewed from a personal, professional or vocational, and a financial position. The answers may not come easily, but only by such an exercise can the titled question of this entire book be seriously considered.

chapter eight

A Look to the Future: Is There Life After Unemployment?

Unemployment brings about a tremendous redirection and reorganization of lives. Personal, vocational, and financial considerations take on new meanings. Before ever finding a new job many vitally important things must be considered to just contend with the potential of a long period of idleness. How will the rent or mortgage payments be made? Where will the money for food come from? Should you consider moving to a new city to find work? These are all very relevant questions and the answers may be difficult to find and even harder to accept. As you begin to assess your own financial capabilities, your actual income may appear to be more than encumbered by the payments required of it. This will mean a forced change in lifestyle that you may be very reluctant to make. But it seems that when confronted with the number of absolute demands made upon a spouse's salary and any unemployment benfits available, no imaginable way can be found to make ends meet. Because of this, some new alternatives have to be explored. For you, these may range from refinancing a mortgage to selling a vehicle to borrowing money from family members. By responding to the questions, "Where am I now?", "Where am I going?", and "How will I get there?", you may begin to realistically evaluate the extent of personal and financial losses and to move in directions to meet the needs of each most effectively.

For instance, financially you need to determine exactly how much monthly income is now available and also how much will be needed to continue to live as you have been. The disparity between these totals will lead to two obvious conclusions. First, you will have to do things to either increase the monthly income substantially. Or, second, you will have to arrange to decrease expenses drastically. How this situation will be corrected, however, may not be clear-cut. While there are some very concrete measures you can take to reduce financial obligations and thus relieve some of this pressure, you should recognize that there is a danger in becoming too comfortable or complacent about being unemployed. Some anxiety in this sense is good because it provides an incentive to return to work and become productive again. I have encountered a few people who have adjusted to the level of income from unemployment or welfare benefits and resolved themselves to not being reemployed. You do not want this to happen to you! The most viable alternatives for you are to: one, change where you live and lower the rent; two, sell a car and get out of a large monthly payment as well as any accompanying expenses, and three, lower food and recreation spending. Although you may be reluctant to do it, life and medical insurance policies may have to be allowed to lapse as the premiums become too difficult to meet. This has become a more prevalent practice for others as well when a period of unemployment persists with little hope of returning to work in the near future. Further considerations forced by financial pressures range from obtaining welfare benefits or food stamps to asking community sources for charity. As uncomfortable as such thoughts are at the time, they are not even comparable to the feelings experienced when they became reality. It is very difficult to maintain any sense of self-worth or dignity under these circumstances. The financial reorganization that becomes necessary during a crisis such as unemployment brings with it the potential for tremendous emotional and psychological pain.

VOCATIONAL CONSIDERATIONS

Realizing that unemployment benefits only last for so long, you should begin as quickly as possible to assess skills and abilities as well as to consider other areas of potential work. Initially, you may hold fast to the belief that you will either pursue a job in only a few select areas or just be self-employed. After a number of months pass with very few prospects of employment, you may start to alter perceptions of what you would be content doing. Thoughts of being self-employed are pleasant if money is being earned and there are many things to do. But if nothing arises from such an endeavor, the benefits of working for someone else seem greatly enhanced. Because of this, you should begin to consider doing any kind of work if it presents the possibility of you earning a fair salary and carries some reasonable expectation that it will last for a while. If you are able to dismiss any belief in the myth that real job security ever exists, you will know that you can only hope to find a stable situation, but you may continue to recognize an inner desire for a job that will be secure for a long time.

Other changes occur that further accent a growing need to work again. Initially, you may not be interested in part-time work. After a prolonged idleness, however, you may consider not only a part-time job but two or even three such jobs at the same time. What once seemed so alien may become very acceptable! In a similar fashion, I had refused to consider moving to another city to find work during the first couple of months, but after that time, my reluctance to leave friends and familiar surroundings disappeared as I sought jobs in other states and cities around the country. This reorganization of not only one life, but the lives of other family members is quickly becoming a prevailing way of life for many people who are unemployed. In search of work, friends are left behind, children must change schools and families are sometimes broken up. It may seem that after spending many weeks and months without a job, just the hope of returning to work regardless of the location, is enough to change some of the most deeply held convictions about family and friends.

PERSONAL CONSIDERATIONS

The effects of unemployment on the personal lives of all family members are very great. Marriages must contend with increasing financial pressures, a strong possibility of being uprooted, and a deep loss of self-esteem on the part of those who have become unemployed. You may be forced to seriously consider the reality that your own marriage might not withstand the separation caused by having to move alone to another locale to find a job. With this in mind, you are confronted with the alternative that if the entire family moved, both your wife and you could be without a job until you find work again. This is a more unsettling thought. If life can go on even minimally with one of you working what would happen if both of you were unemployed for any length of time?

I have seen more than one marriage relationship dissolve under the constant and increasing pressures caused by unemployment. Perhaps some of the break-ups would have occurred anyway, but the catalyst for the ultimate parting was certainly the fact that one person was unemployed and the accompanying sense of failure and hopelessness overwhelmed any chance the marriage had to succeed. More and more often, out-of-work individuals are showing the ill effects of not having a job to go to or not being able to work for a wage. From sexual impotence to alcohol abuse, the family unit has become the primary showcase for the negative fallout of unemployment. Each day that passes as you remain at home with no money coming in, you can see changes occurring. Minor disagreements about what brand of food to buy become major confrontations over money being wasted. While once an inquiry about a day's activities was a sign of genuine interest, it turns into a prying form of interrogation. Defensiveness abounds as each week brings more pressures, both financial and personal.

FUNDAMENTAL CONCERNS

Recognizing that the loss of a job signals the end of any form of security you may have once felt, you must begin to assume new positions and beliefs that focus primarily on the survival of your family and the maintenance of a positive self-concept. As a result of the changes, you begin to realize that you now take fewer chances than you once did. Professionally this may mean that you are less innovative and more concerned with doing things right the first time. Others I have spoken to who have gotten new jobs relate such feelings of being reluctant to speak out or offer new ideas for fear of perhaps being viewed as a rebel or as uncooperative by the boss or owner. In the short term, this may tend to protect a person, but in the long run it only serves to lessen the person's value to a company.

In your personal life, you may become less trusting of others as you strive to protect youself from the pain of possibly losing a friend or being misunderstood. To those who have remained close to you throughout the ordeal of being unemployed, this may not be a very noticeable change because it has not eroded any of the faith you have in them as friends. However, as you encounter new people and begin to interact with them, you will sense a reluctance to share substantive feelings as you protect yourself from any possible negative effects of being so open. You may become aware of a loss of personal dignity or self-worth, and because of this a fear that others may not respect you. Though the realization of this can keep you from becoming an emotional cripple, the struggle to regain self-respect after feeling useless for such a long time must continue.

For many older individuals I have spoken to who are without a job for reasons ranging from early retirement to actually being fired, this kind of personal reorganization has been extremely traumatic. Because they are in the latter stages of their life, these people feel stripped of the personal worth and meaning derived from performing their jobs. Those who recognize the probability of never working again purely because of their age, find life very painful and unsympathetic. By comparison, your own feelings of inadequacy may have never been amplified by a sense of being too old to reenter the work force. In this regard you are much more fortunate than some who have been encouraged to take early retirement or have been *furloughed* after 30 years of service to a company.

Financially, you become very aware of the need to establish some form of regular savings and budget planning. Although you may have paid attention to these things before you became unemployed, after losing your job the importance of them becomes much more apparent. Money takes on such a different meaning when it is so abruptly taken away. Even if you had never considered yourself an extravagant spender, by comparison you may feel like a miser when confronted with the reality of little or no income at all. Financial considerations seem to spill over into so many of the daily activities that you had once taken for granted that you may sometimes wish that you had never bought a home or a car, or had never made friends or grown to enjoy the company of others. At times it may seem that living as a hermit in a single-room apartment would be utopia!

In talking with others who were unemployed, I found that they were very strongly affected by the financial realities of being unemployed. The impact seemed to be due not so much from a concern about food or shelter as it was with being completely and totally without money and unable to even think about small things such as a newspaper, a cup of coffee, or a toy for the children. The futility experienced under such circumstances is immense and it is not a feeling that subsides very easily. One day as I was leaving the job service center, I stopped to talk with someone I had known only slightly. He had hoped to find some work for just a day if possible because his daughter was having a birthday very soon and he wanted to be able to buy a gift for her. The result of his search was apparent in his eyes as he told me his story. Ironically, his pain and disappointment were as difficult for me to handle as my own feelings of inadequacy from not being able to help him. That moment also made me recognize that even if I could have given him some money for the gift, it would have only added to his frustration of being unable to provide the kind of life for his family that he wanted so desperately to provide.

IS THERE LIFE AFTER UNEMPLOYMENT?

The answer to this question is yes—there is life after unemployment. However, the difficult question remains, "What is the quality of life after being unemployed?" To this, there is no simple response. As described already, the effects of losing a job may permeate the total existence of an individual. Husbands, wives, children, parents, friends, neighbors, teachers, and counselors all feel, to some extent, the impact of unemployment. Unfortunately, though there is potential for some positive gains to occur in personal, interpersonal, and vocational areas, this most often is not the case without a hard-fought and lengthy emotional battle.

I would like to believe that my marriage has ultimately been strengthened by this crisis, but I am certain scars remain where there were none before and how this will affect my future I am uncertain. I would also like to think that my friends see me no differently now than they once did, but I have ample evidence to suggest that this is untrue. In this respect, I am aware that I, too, view them differently. Some I am closer with, and with others a distance has been created that may never be resolved.

Many myths that I once perceived as truth have been destroyed. Although it was not good to base beliefs and behaviors on transient or partial truths, the reorganization of values has been a long and sometimes painful ordeal for me. In the process, some fundamental beliefs have been challenged that had once felt very comfortable. Each change in perception brought about a chain reaction of self-doubt, questioning, reassessment, and more change.

Life does go on after unemployment, but it is never the same. After 20 years with a company, there is no way to overcome the feeling of being tossed aside like a piece of disposable hardware. The realization that a company will possibly hire a younger person at half the salary to do the same job only aggravates this feeling. For many people anger and resentment dominate a pool of feelings that had once been largely positive and healthy. These are the kinds of casualties of this war. Youth may help to maintain a vision of hope or optimism and allow negative feelings to be experienced and then released. But there is no bright future for many of the unemployed. There are no tools to combat feelings of despair, hopelessness, futility, or personal inadequacy. As these give way to the emotions of anger and resentment, the realistic possibility of ever being a productive and loyal employee again becomes severely diminished.

To the casual participants in the world of work, being unemployed represents only an inconvenience. They experience little anxiety about personal goals not being met or letting external forces control their life. On the contrary, if the system can make decisions for these individuals, then the system can assume responsibility for feeding and sheltering them. This, too, is an example of a casualty of being unemployed. The loss is measured in human terms of dignity, personal meaning and adequacy, and alienation.

I have been extremely lucky in many ways to have weathered this storm as well as I have. I owe a great deal to a few people who have helped me immeasurably. I know their insights and compassion have gone far in allowing me to be aware of the dangers I have described and the potentials I feel exist within me. At times I try to believe that I could have accomplished everything by myself. But to have reassessed my own skills, values, interests, and abilities, while at the same time remaining acutely aware of the significant changes occurring within me would have been quite a juggling act. I could not have done it alone and I doubt that I could in the future.

Being unemployed does not lend itself to social interaction and personal growth. Life seems fragmented and the feelings of failure overshadow much of the positive self-regard an individual may possess. As the amount of time spent with others is diminished, the opportunities for receiving affirmation of personal worth are also lessened. This vicious circle of behavior is difficult to overcome. To retreat and become reclusive is a common reaction to feeling so defeated. Without others to pull me from my shell, I believe that I would have been consumed by such behavior.

As I survey my life and accept what happened, it is not easy to feel any sense of accomplishment or success in having come through the entire experience. I recognize it may happen to me again, and the likelihood is even greater that it will happen to someone I know or am familiar with. I hope I have the residual strength and understanding to either cope with such an occurrence myself or help others contend with it if they are so affected. I know that each person must draw his or her own personal meaning from a crisis such as this just as I have. My choice was to push on. To work again was my goal, but to reorganize my life was the challenge. For me this took time, patience, and a great deal of changing. Without the change, however, there would be no "life after unemployment."

As I worked with others who were in similar life straits, I became acutely aware of two things. One, there is a tremendous need to express the feelings being experienced and to share the anxiety being dealt with by the unemployed. Two, there is an equal need to understand and work with these people in ways that can foster growth and a healthy return to the mainstream of society. In response to this second need, self-help groups, churches, counselors, or friends can all lend a hand. Jobs alone do not reestablish the lost feelings of security and belongingness brought on by being without a job. It takes time to allow the wounds of unemployment to heal and even with the passage of time, the scars will linger on. Even now, when I enter a room of people, I find myself counting how many are present. Based on current levels of unemployment, I imagine how many of us are being directly affected by this life crisis. By doing this, I am able to quickly realize that I am not alone and there are probably at least one or two others who have either been through or are going through such a period. Facts do dispel myths, and believing that I was the only person who was suffering with thoughts of being a failure or feeling alienated was a myth I shattered by simply talking to other people.

Working or having a job to do is vitally important in fostering a strong feeling of belongingness and personal adequacy. However, with no guarantee of lifetime employment, these things must be nourished in other ways as well. Family members and friends must be allowed to help when it is appropriate. Employment needs must be open to fulfillment through various fields and experiences. Times change, situations change and to contend with these you, too, must change or, at least, demonstrate a flexibility to live differently as time passes. Unemployment will remain a challenge to you even if it is not a personal reality. The challenge is to draw the greatest amount of meaning and satisfaction that you can from the work you do. Second, the challenge is to be able to foster feelings of dignity and self-worth in as many areas of life as possible. These include not only a job, but a family and close friends as well.

When you look back upon all that may have happened, it should become painfully clear that a job is merely a means to an end and something that must be held in clear perspective as it relates to many other equally important considerations in life. You should hope to never again feel as disappointed and helpless as you once did. There is no reward in being angry, hostile, or resentful. Feeling alienated from others is very painful, and considering yourself a failure as an employee and inadequate as a spouse is equally as difficult. You must know that you are capable of surviving such an experience and by sharing your thoughts with others, you will know that you were not and are not alone.

Index

A

Acceptance of loss, 71
Anger:
  as common denominator, 61
  healthy, 73
  internalized, 75
  of others, 73
  repression of, 61

B

Beliefs, 93
Brainstorming, 81
Burnout, 1

C

Catharsis, 79
Challenge, 81
Challenge vs. threat, 67–68, 107
Change, causes of:
  colleagues, 55
  idleness, 56
  salary level, 56
Change in perception:
  honesty, 53
  respect of others, 54
  self-reliance, 55
  values, 52–55
Chauvinism, pervasive, 15
Children, effects on, 17
Concession, period of, 71
Condemnation, period of, 73
Control, period of, 76
Curiosity, 11

D

Danger signals:
  negativism, 106
  procrastination, 106
  self-direction, loss of, 107
Defense mechanisms, use of:
  identification, 77
  projection, 78
  rationalization, 77
  suppression, 78
Denial, 70
  unhealthy, 75
Disassociation, 23
Dispelling myths, 101–102

E

Early retirement, 114
Economic war zone, 22

Emotional assets, 16
Emotional scars, 61
Employer dilemma, 9, 96
Employer statements, 12
Employer-employee relationship, 10
Employment, testing limits, 52
Expressed anger, 73

F

Family, awareness of, 69
Family, informing, 13
Feelings, initial:
  anger, 13
  hostility, 13
  powerlessness, 113
Financial considerations, 11, 110, 114
Financial dependence, 74
Financial security, loss of, 58
Finding work, myth of, 99
First-time offenders, 34
Friends:
  informing, 19
  patronizing, 20
  regrets of, 20
  resources, 86
  role models, 21
Fundamental concerns, 113
Furloughed, 5, 114

G

Government loans, 2
Grieving process, 70

H

Helplessness, feelings of, 15

I

Identification with others, 77
Incorrigibles, 36
Insurance companies, 11
Insurance policies, 58

J

Job referrals, 21
Jobs, myths about, 94
Job security:
  long-term, 89
  loss of, 59, 69

  myth of, 98
  need for, 90

L

Loss of job, causes for, 8

M

Marriage, effects on, 14
Mourning period, 13
Myths, 93, 94, 98, 103
  of competition, 96
  of work quality, 96

N

Need satisfaction:
  acceptance of others, 65
  love, 64
  self-esteem, 64
Negative feelings, misdirected, 76
Negativism, effects of, 77
"Nest eggs", 59
Normalization, 5 C's of, 71–85

P

Parents, effects on, 18
Perception of myths, 95
Personal choices, 66
Personal considerations, 112
Personal losses, 60
Physical abuse, 76
Pink slips, 7
Positive effects, 66
Power, loss of, 14
Powerlessness, 70
Private employment agency, 88
Private placement, 86
Process of denial, 23
Process of normalization, 70
Professional affiliations, 23
Projection, use of, 78
Psychological trauma, 49
Public agencies, 86
Purposelessness, 51

R

Rationalization, 77
Reactions to loss, 8–10
Reemployment, considering, 85
References, obtaining, 87

Reflex tendencies, 88
Relaxing, 63, 64
Reorganization, 70, 79
Resentment, feelings of, 74
Résumé, 87
R.I.F., 5
Risks, taking, 80

S

Sales jobs, considering, 89
Second incomes, 14
Security, loss of, 57, 72
Self-assessment, 69
Self-concept, 75
Self-defense, 63
Self-respect, regaining, 90
Severing ties, 12
Sexual behavior, effects on, 14
Significant others, 49–50
"Snags", 81
Spouse, reactions of anger, 16, 62
Suicide, 105
Support groups, dysfunctional, 32
Suppression, use of, 78
Survival techniques, 43–45
System, The:
  dealing with, 42
  definition of, 26
  during the 70s, 27
  errors in, 44
  learning about, 37
  redemptions of, 47
  shortcomings of, 46
  success within, 27

T

Telephone use, 45
Telling others, 13
Tenure, 5
Tenure, myth of, 94
"Three time losers", 35
"Time bombs", 83
Training, myth of, 99
"Triggers", 82
Trusting, 113

U

Unemployable, 95, 103, 105
Unemployed:
  common denominator, 61
  facts of life of, 30
  vs. unemployable, 103
Unemployment benefits, 7
Unemployment caste system, 33–36
Unemployment, causes of, 10
Unemployment, bad effects of, 50
Unemployment, life after, 115
Unemployment office:
  best days to go, 38–40
  best times to go, 41
  first visit, 29
  other failures, 31
  preconceptions of, 30
Unhealthy perceptions, 105

V

Vocational considerations, 111

W

Wants ads, 86, 89
Want ads, myth of, 99
Wickes Corporation, 2
Work, myths of, 95, 97